How to Build Your

MW01489504

A Complete Guide to Planning, Designing, and
Constructing Your unique Home

Purpose of the Book: How to Build Your Dream Barndominium

The purpose of this book is to empower individuals with the knowledge, confidence, and step by step guidance needed to successfully design and build their own barndominium. Whether you're seeking for a cost-effective housing solution, a unique living space, or a functional combination of home and workshop, this book serves as a comprehensive resource to deal with the entire process.

By breaking down complex construction concepts into approachable and actionable steps, the book aims to:

1. Educate: Provide a clear understanding of what a barndominium is, its advantages, and the key decisions involved in the building process.

2. Inspire: Showcase creative design ideas, and the versatility of barndominiums to motivate you to pursue their dream home.

3. Guide: This book offers practical tools, strategies, and checklists to help you confidently handle planning, budgeting, construction, and maintenance.

4. Solve Problems: Address common challenges, mistakes, and misconceptions, equipping you with solutions to avoid costly pitfalls.

5. Empower: Encourage individuals to take control of their project, whether they want to build it themselves or collaborate with professionals.

Ultimately, this book serves as a trusted companion for anyone from beginners to experienced DIYers looking to transform their vision of a barndominium into a reality, while saving time, money, and effort along the way.

Table of Contents

Chapter 1

Introduction to Barndominium

A barndominium, often called a "barndo," is a hybrid structure that combines the functionality of a barn with the comfort and style of a modern home. Originally used as practical living quarters attached to barns, barndominiums have evolved into versatile and customizable spaces that can serve as homes, workshops, vacation rentals, or multi-purpose properties.

Key Features of a Barndominium

1. Structure: Barndominiums are typically built using metal or wood frames, with durable materials like steel for the exterior walls and roofs.

These structures often feature open floor plans, making them highly adaptable for various layouts and purposes.

2. Dual Functionality: Barndominiums combine residential living spaces with functional areas like workshops, garages, or storage for equipment.

This dual-purpose design makes them ideal for homeowners seeking practicality without compromising comfort.

3. Customization: Unlike traditional homes, barndominiums offer limitless design flexibility. They can be rustic, industrial, or modern, depending on the owner's preferences.

History and Evolution of Barndominiums

The history and evolution of barndominiums is a story of practicality meeting innovation, beginning as a rural necessity and transforming into a popular housing trend. Originally, barndominiums were purely functional structures. Farmers and ranchers often combined their living quarters with barns to stay close to their livestock, equipment, or crops, especially in remote areas where travel between home and work was impractical. These early designs prioritized utility over comfort, often consisting of little more than a basic living space within or attached to a barn. For those working in agriculture, this setup saved time, reduced costs, and provided a way to live and work efficiently on the same property.

The term "barndominium" itself is believed to have been coined in the 1980s by Karl Nilsen, a real estate developer in Connecticut. Nilsen envisioned barndominiums as a new type of community housing, blending barn-like structures with residential living spaces, often for equestrian enthusiasts or those seeking functional, multi-purpose homes near recreational areas. His concept helped spark interest in using barn-style designs for homes, merging practicality with livability. While initially focused on rural applications, this vision marked the beginning of barndominiums transitioning from simple agricultural buildings to versatile spaces with broader appeal.

Over time, barndominiums began evolving beyond their agricultural roots. Advances in construction techniques, materials, and design preferences allowed homeowners to transform these basic structures into fully customizable, modern homes. Steel frames, in particular, became a popular choice for their durability and ease of construction, enabling faster build times and more open floor plans. This adaptability attracted a new demographic of homeowners who saw the potential for barndominiums to meet a wide range of needs, from family homes to workshops, vacation properties, and even commercial spaces.

The 21st century has brought a surge in the popularity of barndominiums, driven by rising housing costs, changing lifestyles, and the growing interest in non-traditional homes. People are increasingly drawn to their affordability, sustainability, and design flexibility. Television programs and online communities have also played a major role in promoting the barndominium lifestyle, showcasing their potential for both luxurious interiors and practical functionality. Today, barndominiums are no longer confined to rural areas; they are being built in suburban and even urban settings, proving their versatility and appeal to a wide range of homeowners.

From humble beginnings as practical structures for farmers to modern, stylish homes that blend rustic charm with contemporary convenience, barndominiums have undergone a remarkable transformation. Their history reflects not only their evolution in design and purpose but also the changing values and needs of homeowners seeking spaces that balance function, affordability, and individuality.

Benefits of Barndominiums

Barndominiums have surged in popularity due to their unique blend of affordability, durability, versatility, and eco-friendliness. These qualities make them a practical and attractive option for modern homeowners seeking a functional yet stylish living space. Let's explore each of these benefits in detail:

1. Affordability

One of the biggest advantages of building a barndominium is its cost-effectiveness compared to traditional homes.

a. Lower Construction Costs: Barndominiums often use pre-fabricated materials like steel, which are cheaper and faster to assemble than conventional construction materials like brick or wood.

- Open floor plans reduce the need for costly structural reinforcements.

b. Reduced Labor Costs: The simplicity of barndominium construction means fewer hours of labor are required, saving on contractor expenses.

- DIY enthusiasts can take on parts of the construction process, further cutting costs.

c. Long-Term Savings: Durable materials, such as metal siding and roofing, reduce maintenance and repair costs over time.

- Energy-efficient designs lead to lower utility bills.

2. Durability

Barndominiums are designed to withstand harsh environmental conditions, making them an excellent choice for long-term living.

a. Weather Resistance: Steel and metal frames provide superior protection against wind, rain, snow, and even extreme weather like hurricanes and tornadoes.

- Metal roofing resists damage from hail and other elements better than traditional shingles.

b. Pest Resistance: Unlike wood-framed homes, barndominiums are impervious to pests such as termites, which can cause significant damage to traditional homes.

c. Fire Resistance: Metal construction materials are less flammable than wood, reducing the risk of fire damage.

d. Longevity: With proper maintenance, barndominiums can last for decades, often outlasting traditional homes.

3. Versatility

Barndominiums offer unmatched flexibility in both design and function, making them suitable for a variety of needs.

a. Customizable Layouts: Open floor plans allow homeowners to design their spaces to fit their unique lifestyles, whether they need a cozy home, a large family space, or multi-purpose areas.

- They can combine living areas with functional spaces like workshops, garages, studios, or storage facilities.

b. Multi-Purpose Use: Barndominiums can serve as homes, vacation rentals, event venues, or even commercial properties.

- Hobbyists, artists, or entrepreneurs can create spaces that combine living areas with work or creative studios.

c. Expansion Options: Adding new rooms, outdoor living spaces, or functional areas (like a barn or garage) is easier due to the modular nature of barndominiums.

4. Eco-Friendliness

Barndominiums can be designed with sustainability in mind, helping homeowners reduce their environmental impact.

a. Energy Efficiency: Steel structures and metal roofs reflect heat, reducing the need for air conditioning in warmer climates.

- High-quality insulation ensures minimal energy loss, keeping heating and cooling costs low.

b. Sustainable Materials: Recycled steel and metal are often used in construction, making barndominiums more environmentally friendly.

- Wood alternatives or repurposed materials can further minimize the environmental footprint.

5. Solar and Renewable Energy Options: Barndominiums are ideal for integrating solar panels, geothermal heating, and other renewable energy systems.

a. Low Waste Construction: Pre-fabricated building kits reduce on-site waste compared to traditional construction methods.

Common Misconceptions About Barndominiums Debunked

Barndominiums have gained significant attention in recent years, but along with their growing popularity, several misconceptions have emerged. Let's address and debunk some of the most common myths to give you a clear and accurate understanding of what barndominiums truly offer.

Misconception 1: "It's just a barn you live in."

The Truth:

While the name "barndominium" suggests a barn-like structure, modern barndominiums are far from rustic barns with haylofts. They can be as luxurious and stylish as any traditional home, with high-end finishes, modern amenities, and sophisticated interiors. The "barn" aspect primarily refers to the structural design or materials, not the living experience.

Why People Believe This:

The term "barndominium" originates from combining "barn" and "condominium," leading to the assumption that it's literally a barn. Early designs were simple and practical, reinforcing this image.

Misconception 2: "Barndominiums are not durable."

The Truth:

Barndominiums are often built with steel frames and metal roofs, making them more durable than many traditional homes. They are designed to withstand extreme weather conditions, including hurricanes, heavy snowfall, and strong winds. Additionally, metal construction makes them resistant to pests like termites and less susceptible to fire.

Why People Believe This:

Since barndominiums are sometimes associated with agricultural buildings, people mistakenly think they are temporary or flimsy structures.

Misconception 3: "They're cheap, so they must look cheap."

The Truth:

Barndominiums are affordable, but that doesn't mean they lack quality or style. In fact, they can be customized with upscale finishes like hardwood floors, granite countertops, custom cabinetry, and vaulted ceilings. The exterior can also be designed to reflect various architectural styles, including modern, rustic, and industrial aesthetics.

Why People Believe This:

The affordability of barndominiums leads some to equate them with low-quality or bare-bones construction. However, cost savings often come from faster build times and efficient materials, not a sacrifice in quality.

Misconception 4: "Barndominiums are only for rural areas."

The Truth:

While barndominiums are popular in rural areas due to ample space and zoning flexibility, they are increasingly being built in suburban and even urban locations. With creative design and proper planning, barndominiums can fit seamlessly into a variety of settings.

Why People Believe This:

The association with barns naturally connects barndominiums to rural environments. Additionally, larger plots of land are often needed for traditional barn-style barndominiums, but modern designs have adapted for smaller lots.

Misconception 5: "Barndominiums don't have good resale value."

The Truth:

Barndominiums can have excellent resale value, especially as they gain mainstream popularity. Buyers are often drawn to their durability, energy efficiency, and unique designs. Well-maintained barndominiums in desirable locations can be just as valuable as traditional homes, if not more so.

Why People Believe This:

The novelty of barndominiums leads to skepticism about their long-term value. However, as they become more common and accepted, their resale potential continues to grow.

Misconception 6: "They're hard to insure or finance."

The Truth:

While securing financing or insurance for a barndominium might have been challenging in the past, it has become much easier as their popularity grows. Many banks and insurance companies now recognize barndominiums as legitimate residential properties. Working with lenders or insurers experienced in non-traditional homes can simplify the process.

Why People Believe This:

Early adopters of barndominiums often struggled to find financing or insurance due to the unconventional nature of these homes. However, increasing demand has led to more options for buyers.

Misconception 7: "Barndominiums aren't energy efficient."

The Truth:

Barndominiums can be extremely energy efficient when properly designed. Metal construction provides excellent insulation options, and many barndominium owners incorporate energy-saving features like solar panels, energy-efficient windows, and geothermal heating. The simplicity of their design also reduces energy waste.

Why People Believe This:

People mistakenly think large, open spaces and metal exteriors make barndominiums hard to heat or cool. However, modern insulation techniques and energy-conscious designs address these concerns effectively.

Misconception 8: "They're difficult to customize."

The Truth:

One of the greatest advantages of barndominiums is their flexibility. Open floor plans allow for nearly limitless customization, making it easy to adapt the design to fit specific needs, from modern family homes to spacious workshops or unique hybrid spaces.

Why People Believe This:

The simplicity of barndominium kits may give the impression that customization options are limited, but these kits are only the starting point. With the right vision and resources, barndominiums can be tailored to any style or purpose.

Note: Barndominiums are versatile, durable, and stylish structures that offer significant advantages over traditional homes. While misconceptions exist, most are based on outdated ideas or limited understanding of the modern capabilities of barndominiums. By debunking these myths, it becomes clear that barndominiums are an innovative and practical housing solution for a wide range of homeowners.

Chapter 2

Check If Barndominium Right for You

Choosing to build a barndominium is a significant decision, and it's important to determine whether this unique type of home aligns with your lifestyle, needs, and preferences. Barndominiums offer many benefits, but they also come with specific considerations that may not suit everyone. Understanding what makes barndominiums appealing, as well as their potential limitations, can help you decide if this innovative housing solution is right for you.

Barndominiums are ideal for people who value flexibility, functionality, and affordability in their homes. With open floor plans and customizable designs, they can be tailored to suit a wide range of lifestyles, from families seeking spacious living quarters to hobbyists or professionals needing integrated workspaces. If you're someone who enjoys rural living, or if you want a property that combines living space with room for workshops, garages, or even animals, a barndominium could be the perfect fit. Their affordability, especially compared to traditional homes, also makes them an excellent option for budget-conscious homeowners or those looking for alternative housing solutions.

One of the biggest appeals of barndominiums is their versatility. Whether you want a modern, minimalist aesthetic, a rustic retreat, or a functional combination of home and workspace, a barndominium can meet your needs. These structures are especially popular among people who want to design a home that reflects their personality or accommodates unique requirements. The open floor plans provide endless possibilities for layout and design, making barndominiums particularly attractive for those who prioritize creative freedom.

However, barndominiums may not be suitable for everyone. If you prefer a traditional home design with separate, defined spaces, the open floor plans that barndominiums are known for might not appeal to you. Similarly, while they are increasingly popular in suburban and urban areas, zoning laws and building codes may make it more challenging to construct one in certain locations. It's essential to research local regulations before deciding if a barndominium is feasible for your property.

Another factor to consider is climate. Barndominiums, often constructed with steel frames and metal siding, can require special insulation to regulate temperatures in extreme climates. If you live in an area with particularly harsh winters or scorching summers, you'll need to invest in proper insulation, heating, and cooling systems to ensure year-round comfort.

If you enjoy DIY projects, a barndominium might be a rewarding choice, as many homeowners take an active role in building or customizing their spaces. Pre-fabricated kits make the construction process easier and more accessible, even for those with minimal construction experience. On the other hand, if you prefer to rely entirely on professionals, you'll need to ensure that your contractors have experience with this specific type of build.

Finally, think about your long-term goals. Barndominiums are incredibly durable and low-maintenance, making them a great option for those who want a home that will stand the test of time. They're also adaptable, which means you can expand or modify them as your needs change. Whether you're starting a family, downsizing, or looking for a multi-purpose property, a barndominium can evolve with you.

Chapter 3

Setting a Realistic Budget for Your Barndominium

Building a barndominium is often more affordable than constructing a traditional home, but like any major project, it requires careful financial planning. Setting a realistic budget is critical to ensure that your barndominium meets your needs without unexpected costs derailing your plans. With the right approach, you can enjoy the cost-effective benefits of a barndominium while avoiding common budgeting mistakes.

1. Understand the Total Costs Involved

The first step in setting your budget is understanding all the components that contribute to the total cost of building a barndominium. While barndominiums are known for being cost-efficient, their final price depends on several factors:

Construction Costs: This includes the foundation, framing, roof, walls, and exterior materials, such as metal or wood. Depending on the size and materials you choose, this can range between \$50 and \$150 per square foot.

Interior Finishing: Flooring, walls, cabinetry, lighting, plumbing, and HVAC systems can significantly impact your budget. These costs vary widely based on whether you opt for basic finishes or high-end features.

Land Costs: If you don't already own land, purchasing property will add to your budget. Land prices vary greatly depending on location, zoning, and amenities like utilities or road access.

Site Preparation: Clearing, grading, and preparing the land for construction can also add to the overall cost, especially if extensive work is needed.

Permits and Fees: You'll need to account for local building permits, inspections, and zoning fees. Research your area's requirements to include these in your budget.

Utilities: Installing water, electricity, and sewage systems on undeveloped land can be a significant expense. If you're in a remote area, off-grid solutions like solar panels or septic tanks may increase costs.

Furniture and Décor: Don't forget to budget for the furniture, appliances, and décor needed to make your barndominium livable.

Having these factors in mind, you'll have a clearer picture of the total expenses involved and can set a realistic budget that accounts for both the expected and the unexpected.

2. Determine Your Priorities

A barndominium's versatility allows for many design and material options, so determining your priorities early on will help you allocate your budget effectively. Ask yourself:

- Do you want a large, spacious home, or is a compact design sufficient?
- Are high-end finishes and customizations important, or are you content with basic options?
- Will you need extra spaces, such as workshops, garages, or storage areas?

Focusing on what matters most to you will help you balance your budget and make decisions that align with your goals.

3. Account for Hidden and Unexpected Costs

Unexpected expenses are common in construction projects, so it's essential to build a buffer into your budget. These costs might include:

- Unforeseen site preparation challenges, such as poor soil conditions or drainage issues.
- Rising material prices, which can fluctuate based on market conditions.

- Changes to your design or materials during construction (commonly known as "scope creep").
- Additional costs for permits or inspections if there are delays or adjustments to the plan.

Expert tip: It is recommended setting aside 10–20% of your total budget as a contingency fund to cover these surprises.

4. Consider Financing Options

If you're unable to pay for your barndominium entirely out of pocket, financing options can help you move forward with the project. Many lenders now offer loans specifically for barndominiums, including construction loans and mortgages for completed properties. Before committing, ensure you understand:

- The interest rates and terms associated with the loan.

- How much of the cost the lender will cover and whether you'll need to make a down payment.
- Any requirements, such as appraisals or inspections, needed to secure financing.

Choosing a reputable lender with experience in barndominium projects will make the process smoother and help you stay within your budget.

5. Balance DIY vs. Professional Costs

One of the unique aspects of building a barndominium is the opportunity to take on parts of the project yourself. From painting to installing flooring or even assembling pre-fabricated kits, a DIY approach can save money. However, it's important to know your limits attempting tasks beyond your skill level can lead to costly mistakes. Hiring professionals for critical areas, such as foundation work, framing, and utility installation, is often the safest and most cost-effective choice.

Steps to Build a Realistic Budget

1. Research Costs Thoroughly: Gather quotes from builders, contractors, and suppliers in your area. Use online tools and resources to estimate the cost of materials and labor.

2. Create a Detailed Plan: Finalize your floor plan and design choices before starting construction to minimize costly changes.

3. Track Expenses: Use budgeting software or spreadsheets to monitor spending and ensure you stay on track throughout the project.

4. Prepare for the Unexpected: Factor in a contingency fund for unforeseen expenses.

Why a Realistic Budget Matters

Setting a realistic budget isn't just about avoiding financial stress—it's about ensuring your dream barndominium becomes a reality. By thoroughly researching costs, prioritizing what matters most, and planning for the unexpected, you'll be able to

build a home that fits your needs and stays within your financial means. With the right approach, your barndominium project can be a rewarding and cost-effective journey that delivers lasting satisfaction.

Chapter 4

Choosing the Right Location for Your Barndominium

Selecting the perfect location for your barndominium is one of the most critical decisions in the building process. The land you choose will determine not only the functionality of your home but also its long-term value, accessibility, and overall suitability for your lifestyle. By carefully considering factors such as zoning, utilities, environment, and future needs, you can ensure your location aligns with your vision for your barndominium.

1. Assess Your Needs and Lifestyle

Before searching for land, consider how your location will impact your day-to-day life. Are you looking for a rural retreat, a suburban property, or a space that offers both work and living areas? Think about the following questions:

- Do you need room for additional structures like a workshop, garage, or barn?
- Will you require space for outdoor activities, farming, or livestock?
- How important is proximity to schools, workplaces, or community services?

When you identify your priorities, you can narrow your search to areas that best suit your lifestyle and goals.

2. Understand Zoning Laws and Building Codes

Zoning laws and building codes vary widely depending on location, and they play a major role in determining whether you can build a barndominium on a particular piece of land. Some areas may restrict the type of construction allowed, while others may require specific permits or inspections.

Key considerations include:

- Zoning Designations: Confirm whether the land is zoned for residential, agricultural, or mixed-use purposes. Barndominiums are often ideal for agricultural or mixed-use zones but may face restrictions in certain residential areas.
- Setback Requirements: Many municipalities require structures to be built a certain distance from property lines, roads, or other buildings.
- Height and Size Limits: Some areas impose restrictions on building height or square footage.
- Homeowners' Associations (HOAs): If the property is part of an HOA, review their rules to ensure your barndominium plans comply.

Note: Before purchasing land, consult with local authorities or a land-use attorney to avoid costly surprises later in the process.

3. Evaluate Utilities and Infrastructure

The availability of utilities and infrastructure can significantly impact the cost and feasibility of building a barndominium. Assess the following:

- Water Supply: Determine whether the property has access to municipal water or if you'll need to drill a well.
- Electricity: Check for nearby power lines or consider alternative options like solar power if the location is remote.
- Sewage and Waste Disposal: Decide whether the land connects to a sewer system or if you'll need to install a septic system.
- Road Access: Ensure the property has a reliable access road, especially if it's in a rural area. Gravel or dirt roads may require upgrades to handle construction equipment.

- Internet and Communication: For those working from home or relying on connectivity, confirm the availability of high-speed internet and cell phone coverage.

Note that the cost of extending utilities or creating infrastructure on undeveloped land can add significantly to your overall budget, so include these considerations when evaluating potential sites.

4. Consider the Environmental Factors

Environmental conditions can influence both the construction and long-term maintenance of your barndominium. Take time to assess the property's natural features and how they might affect your build:

- Soil Quality: Poor soil conditions may require expensive foundation work or grading. A soil test can help determine the land's suitability for building.

- Flood Risk: Check FEMA flood maps to ensure the land is not in a floodplain or prone to water damage. If the area has a flood risk, additional precautions like elevated foundations may be necessary.
- Climate: Evaluate how the local climate will impact your barndominium's insulation, heating, and cooling needs. For instance, areas with extreme heat or cold may require additional investments in energy efficiency.
- Topography: Flat land is typically easier and cheaper to build on, while hilly or uneven terrain may require grading or retaining walls.
- Natural Hazards: Consider risks such as tornadoes, hurricanes, or wildfires, and plan for mitigation measures if needed.

Knowing the land's environmental conditions, you can design a barndominium that not only meets your needs but also stands the test of time.

5. Proximity to Amenities

The ideal location balances your desire for privacy with access to essential services and amenities. While rural areas are popular for barndominiums, it's important to think about how far you're willing to travel for basic necessities. Consider:

- Grocery stores, gas stations, and medical facilities.
- Schools, workplaces, and community centers if you're raising a family.
- Hardware stores and suppliers for ongoing maintenance or DIY projects.
- Recreational opportunities like parks, lakes, or trails if outdoor activities are important to you.

If you're building a barndominium as an income property or vacation rental, proximity to tourist attractions or unique features can boost its appeal and profitability.

6. Future Growth and Resale Value

Choosing a location isn't just about the present it's also an investment in the future. Consider the potential for property value appreciation and whether the land will still meet your needs years down the road. Look at factors like:

- Local development plans that may increase the area's appeal or convenience.
- Neighborhood growth and infrastructure improvements that could boost property values.
- The potential for expanding or upgrading your barndominium as your needs evolve.

Resale value is another important consideration, especially if you might sell the property later. Barndominiums are growing in popularity, but they may appeal more to certain buyers, such as those who value rural living or multi-functional spaces. Choosing a desirable location will make your property more marketable in the future.

Note: Choosing the right location is a blend of practicality, planning, and personal preference. Whether you're looking for a quiet retreat surrounded by nature or a convenient spot near amenities, the ideal property will provide the foundation for your dream barndominium. Take the time to research and evaluate potential sites thoroughly, and don't hesitate to seek expert advice when necessary. With the right location, your barndominium will not only meet your current needs but also offer long-term satisfaction and value.

Chapter 5

Creating a Vision for Your Barndominium

Building a barndominium begins with a vision a clear and inspiring idea of what you want your future home to look like and how it will serve your needs. This step is critical because it lays the foundation for every decision you'll make during the planning and construction process. Whether you dream of a cozy retreat, a functional live-work space, or a spacious family home, crafting a detailed vision will ensure your barndominium reflects your lifestyle, priorities, and personal style.

1. Define Your Purpose and Priorities

The first step in creating your vision is to identify the primary purpose of your barndominium. Think about how you plan to use the space and what features are most important to you. Are you looking for a full-time residence, a vacation home, or a combination of living and workspaces?

Perhaps you need room for hobbies, a workshop, or even storage for equipment or vehicles.

Next, consider your priorities. What elements are non-negotiable for your dream home? For example:

- Do you want an open floor plan to create a sense of spaciousness?
- Will you need additional functional spaces like a garage, barn, or office?
- Are energy efficiency and sustainability key goals for your project?

2. Envision the Layout and Functionality

Barndominiums are known for their flexibility, so take advantage of the opportunity to create a layout that perfectly suits your needs. Start by imagining how you'll use the space daily. Consider the number of bedrooms, bathrooms, and shared spaces you'll need, as well as how these areas will flow together.

For example, families may prioritize large kitchens, communal living spaces, and private bedrooms, while someone building a live-work space might focus on integrating an office or workshop with the living area. Think about your routines, hobbies, and future plans, and make sure the layout accommodates them.

When planning functionality, consider the following:

- Zones for Living and Work: Do you need separate areas for relaxation, productivity, and hobbies?
- Storage Solutions: Will you need storage for tools, equipment, or recreational items?
- Flexibility for the Future: Can the layout adapt to changes, like adding new rooms or repurposing spaces?

3. Incorporate Style and Aesthetics

The beauty of a barndominium is its versatility in design you can make it as rustic or modern as you like. Your vision should include the overall aesthetic you want to achieve, both inside and out. Do you picture a sleek, minimalist design with clean lines and neutral colors, or do you prefer a cozy, farmhouse-inspired look with wood beams and warm finishes?

Consider the following elements to shape your style:

- Exterior Design: Choose materials and colors for the outside of your barndominium. Popular options include metal siding, wood accents, and large windows to enhance natural light.
- Interior Finishes: Think about flooring, countertops, cabinetry, and lighting. These details can transform a basic structure into a space that feels uniquely yours.

- Architectural Features: Add personality with vaulted ceilings, loft spaces, or oversized sliding doors.

Collect inspiration from home design websites, magazines, to create a mood board that captures the look and feel you're aiming for.

4. Incorporate Inspiration from Other Designs

If you're feeling stuck, looking at examples of other barndominiums can be incredibly helpful. Explore design blogs, social media groups, and builder portfolios to see what others have done. Pay attention to features or layouts that stand out to you, and note any design elements you'd like to replicate or modify.

Some popular barndominium styles include:

- Modern Industrial: Sleek metal accents, concrete floors, and open spaces.
- Rustic Farmhouse: Wood beams, shiplap walls, and warm, earthy tones.

- Contemporary Minimalist: Neutral colors, simple lines, and a focus on functionality.
- Hybrid Designs: A mix of styles that blend elements of modern and rustic for a personalized touch.

5. Account for Practicalities

While dreaming up your ideal barndominium is exciting, it's essential to keep practicalities in mind. Your vision should align with your budget, location, and lifestyle. For example, if you're building in a cold climate, energy-efficient insulation and heating systems should be part of your plan. Similarly, if your budget is limited, prioritize high-impact features and finishes while considering cost-saving alternatives for less critical areas.

Here are some practical aspects to consider:

- Building Size: Ensure the square footage meets your needs without exceeding your budget.
- Energy Efficiency: Plan for insulation, windows, and energy-efficient systems that reduce long-term costs.
- Maintenance: Choose materials that are durable and easy to maintain, like metal siding and roofing.
- Local Codes and Regulations: Ensure your design complies with zoning laws and building codes in your area.

6. Visualize Your Outdoor Space

Your barndominium's location and outdoor area are just as important as the interior. Envision how you'll use the land surrounding your home. Will you need a large yard, a garden, or space for animals? Do you want outdoor entertaining areas like a patio, porch, or fire pit?

Consider how the exterior of your barndominium will blend with the environment. Natural landscaping, driveways, fencing, and pathways all contribute to the overall vision of your property.

7. Put Your Vision into Action

Once you've created a clear vision for your barndominium, document it thoroughly. Create sketches, mood boards, or a design notebook that captures your ideas in one place. This will serve as a roadmap for your project, helping you communicate your goals to builders, contractors, or designers.

- Your vision should strike a balance between creativity and practicality. With a well-thought-out plan, you'll be able to turn your dream barndominium into a home that reflects your style, supports your lifestyle, and brings your ideas to life.

Chapter 6

Deciding on DIY vs. Hiring Professionals for Your Barndominium

One of the most important decisions you'll face when building a barndominium is whether to take a DIY approach, hire professionals, or combine the two. Each option has its benefits and challenges, and the best choice depends on your skill level, budget, time availability, and the complexity of the project. To make an informed decision, it's crucial to weigh the pros and cons of each approach and understand how they align with your specific goals.

A. Weighing the Pros and Cons of Building It Yourself vs. Hiring Contractors

When deciding how to approach your barndominium project, it's essential to weigh the advantages and challenges of building it yourself (DIY) versus hiring contractors. Both options offer unique benefits, but they also come with trade-offs that can impact your timeline, budget, and overall experience. To help you make an informed decision, let's explore the pros and cons of each approach.

Building It Yourself (DIY)

Pros

1. Cost Savings

By taking on much of the labor yourself, you can significantly reduce costs, as labor typically accounts for a substantial portion of construction expenses.

- Eliminates contractor markups on materials and services.

2. Creative Freedom

You have full control over every aspect of the build, from design decisions to material selection, ensuring your barndominium reflects your unique vision.

- Adjustments can be made on the fly without consulting or waiting for contractors.

3. Sense of Accomplishment

Successfully building your own home is a rewarding experience. It offers a sense of pride and achievement that comes from turning your vision into reality.

4. Flexibility in Timeline

You can work at your own pace, spreading out the build to fit your schedule and budget, avoiding the pressure of meeting contractor deadlines.

Cons

1. Lack of Expertise

Tasks like framing, wiring, plumbing, and HVAC installation require specialized knowledge. Mistakes can lead to safety hazards, delays, or costly repairs.

- If you lack experience, the quality of work may not match professional standards.

2. Time-Consuming

Building a barndominium yourself requires a significant time investment, often stretching the project timeline by months or even years.

- Juggling work, family, and the build can be overwhelming.

3. Tool and Equipment Costs

DIY requires access to construction tools and heavy equipment. If you don't already own these, renting or purchasing them can add to costs.

4. Navigating Permits and Regulations

Ensuring compliance with building codes, zoning laws, and obtaining permits can be confusing and time-intensive for first-time builders.

5. Risk of Cost Overruns

Without professional oversight, unforeseen issues (e.g., structural miscalculations or wasted materials) can escalate costs.

One thing you should note is that DIY is ideal for those with construction experience, a desire to save money, and the patience to dedicate time and energy to the project. It's especially suitable for simple builds or when using a pre-fabricated barndominium kit.

Hiring Contractors

Pros

1. Expertise and Efficiency

Contractors bring years of experience, ensuring high-quality work that meets safety and building standards.

Their knowledge speeds up the process, often completing the build in a fraction of the time it would take a DIY builder.

2. Access to Resources

Contractors have established relationships with suppliers and can often secure materials at lower costs.

They bring the necessary tools, equipment, and skilled labor for specialized tasks.

3. Peace of Mind

Professional contractors handle all the technical aspects, including permits, inspections, and compliance with building codes.

- You're less likely to encounter costly mistakes or construction delays.

4. Time Savings

Hiring professionals allows you to focus on other priorities in your life while they manage the project.

- They work on a set timeline, which can help complete your barndominium more quickly.

5. Liability and Warranties

Licensed contractors typically offer warranties on their work and materials.

- If something goes wrong, they are responsible for addressing the issue, reducing your financial risk.

Cons

1. Higher Costs

Contractors charge for their labor, project management, and sometimes add markups to materials, significantly increasing the overall cost of the project.

- Unexpected changes or delays can lead to additional expenses.

2. Less Control

While contractors aim to follow your vision, some decisions may need to be delegated, potentially leading to compromises on certain design or material preferences.

3. Finding the Right Contractor

Hiring reliable and experienced contractors can be challenging. Poor communication, lack of experience with barndominiums, or mismanagement can lead to unsatisfactory results.

- Vetting contractors and negotiating contracts requires time and due diligence.

4. Dependence on Their Schedule

Contractors often have multiple projects in progress. If your project isn't their top priority, delays could occur.

5. Less Hands-On Involvement

For homeowners who enjoy a hands-on approach, outsourcing the project can feel less personal or rewarding.

Also note that hiring contractors is good but hiring contractors is ideal for those with larger budgets, limited time, or little construction experience. It's the best option for complex builds or when you want to ensure a high-quality, professional result.

Making the Decision

Key Factors to Consider

1. Your Skill Level: Do you have the knowledge and experience to handle construction tasks safely and effectively?

2. Budget: Can you afford to hire contractors, or would saving on labor allow you to achieve your vision within your financial constraints?

3. Time Availability: Do you have the time to dedicate to a DIY build, or would hiring contractors allow for quicker completion?

4. Complexity of the Build: Is your barndominium a simple design that you can manage, or does it

involve complex systems that require professional expertise?

5. Your Goals and Priorities: Do you value the hands-on experience of building your own home, or do you prioritize efficiency and professional results?

Blending the Two: A Hybrid Approach

If you're torn between the DIY and contractor approach, consider a **"hybrid model"**, where you take on tasks you're confident in (e.g., painting, flooring, or landscaping) and hire professionals for more technical aspects (e.g., foundation, framing, plumbing, and electrical). This can provide the best of both worlds cost savings and professional expertise while allowing you to remain actively involved in the project.

Note: Both DIY and hiring contractors have distinct advantages and challenges. The right choice depends on your skills, budget, time, and

the complexity of your barndominium build. A DIY
project can save money and provide a rewarding
experience, but it demands significant time, effort,
and expertise. Hiring contractors ensures
efficiency and professional quality but comes at a
higher cost and with less hands-on control. By
carefully evaluating your circumstances and goals,
you can choose the approach or combination of
approaches that best suits your needs, ultimately
leading to a barndominium that fulfills your vision
and lifestyle.

B. Understanding Your Skill Level and Limits

When embarking on a barndominium build,
understanding your skill level and limits is
essential to ensure a successful project. While the
idea of constructing your own home can be
exciting and rewarding, it's important to recognize
which tasks you can confidently handle and which
might require professional expertise. Taking on
more than you're prepared for can lead to costly

mistakes, safety hazards, and unnecessary stress. On the other hand, knowing your strengths can help you save money, remain actively involved, and bring your vision to life.

1. Assessing Your Current Skills

Start by evaluating your knowledge and experience in construction and home-building tasks. Ask yourself the following questions:

- Do you have prior experience with similar projects? Have you ever completed a significant DIY project, such as building furniture, remodeling a room, or constructing a shed? Experience with even small-scale construction can give you a foundation to build on.
- Are you familiar with construction techniques and terminology? Do you understand the basics of framing, roofing, insulation, or finishing work? Being

comfortable with these processes is crucial for tackling more advanced tasks.

- Do you know how to read blueprints or design plans? Interpreting technical drawings is key to ensuring accuracy during construction. If this is outside your expertise, you may need help from a professional or detailed pre-designed plans.

- Do you have knowledge of local building codes and permits? Compliance with regulations is mandatory. Mistakes here can result in fines, delays, or unsafe construction.

2. Evaluating Your Physical Capabilities

Building a barndominium is physically demanding. Consider whether you're equipped to handle tasks that involve:

- Heavy lifting (e.g., framing materials or metal panels).

- Working at heights (e.g., roofing or installing loft spaces).
- Repetitive and labor-intensive tasks like digging, pouring concrete, or installing drywall.

If you have any physical limitations or health concerns, be realistic about what you can safely do and where you may need assistance.

3. Time Commitment

Another crucial factor is the amount of time you can dedicate to the project.

- Do you have the flexibility to work on the build regularly, or will you be limited by a full-time job or family responsibilities?
- Complex tasks like framing, electrical, and plumbing often require weeks or months of focused effort. If your time is limited, you may need to prioritize simpler DIY tasks and outsource the rest.

- Delays caused by insufficient time can stretch the project timeline and increase costs for things like equipment rentals or contractor availability.

4. Safety Knowledge and Concerns

Construction involves inherent risks, and safety should always be a top priority. Evaluate whether you have:

- Knowledge of proper safety procedures (e.g., using power tools, working on ladders, or handling sharp materials).
- Access to safety equipment, such as gloves, goggles, and hard hats.
- Confidence to manage tasks that involve electrical systems, gas lines, or structural stability—areas where mistakes can lead to serious injuries or hazards.

If you lack experience in these areas, hiring professionals or seeking guidance is highly recommended.

5. Tasks You Might Handle Yourself

If you have basic construction skills or are willing to learn, there are several tasks you might confidently tackle on your own:

- Painting and Finishing: Interior and exterior painting are manageable for most people and can save a significant amount of money.
- Flooring Installation: Laminate, vinyl, or even hardwood floors can be installed by DIYers with some patience and research.
- Landscaping: Designing and implementing outdoor spaces around your barndominium is a great DIY project.
- Assembling Pre-Fabricated Kits: Many barndominium kits are designed for assembly by homeowners with basic tools and skills.

6. Tasks Best Left to Professionals

For complex or highly technical aspects of the build, professional assistance is often necessary to ensure safety and compliance with building codes:

- Foundation Work: Pouring a level and secure foundation is critical for the stability of your barndominium.
- Framing and Structural Elements: Mistakes in framing can compromise the structural integrity of the building.
- Plumbing and Electrical Systems: These require specialized skills and certifications to ensure safety and code compliance.
- Roof Installation: Working on a roof involves both safety risks and precision to prevent leaks or other issues.
- HVAC Systems: Proper installation of heating, ventilation, and air conditioning systems requires professional expertise for energy efficiency and long-term reliability.

7. Recognizing When to Seek Help

Understanding your limits doesn't mean you can't take on new challenges, but it's important to know when to ask for help. If you encounter a task that feels overwhelming, don't hesitate to:

- Consult professionals for advice or partial assistance.
- Take a course or watch tutorials to improve your knowledge.
- Hire a contractor for specific phases of the build, such as framing, wiring, or plumbing.

Seeking help when necessary will save you time, reduce stress, and ensure your barndominium is built safely and correctly.

8. Building Confidence with a Learning Mindset

If you're new to construction but eager to take on a DIY project, there are plenty of ways to build your skills:

- Research thoroughly using books, online videos, and tutorials.
- Practice with smaller projects, like building furniture or a shed, before taking on major construction tasks.
- Work alongside experienced builders or volunteers to gain hands-on experience.

A willingness to learn can expand your skillset and help you feel more prepared for larger tasks.

C. The Role of Professionals

When building a barndominium, professionals like architects, engineers, builders, and interior designers play critical roles in ensuring your project is safe, efficient, and aligned with your vision. While it's possible to take on certain aspects of the process yourself, relying on experienced professionals for key stages of the project can save time, minimize costly mistakes, and deliver a superior result. Here's an overview of how these experts contribute to the success of your barndominium build.

Architects: The Visionaries of Your Barndominium

Architects are responsible for turning your ideas into a tangible design. They focus on both the functionality and aesthetics of your barndominium, ensuring the structure meets your needs, complements your style, and complies with local building codes.

Key Responsibilities:

1. Design and Layout:

- Architects create detailed floor plans, elevations, and blueprints that balance your vision with practicality.
- They help determine the optimal layout of rooms, flow between spaces, and overall structure.

2. Customization: They tailor designs to meet your specific needs, such as incorporating unique features (e.g., loft spaces, large open areas, or multi-use rooms).

3. Code Compliance: Architects ensure the design adheres to zoning laws, building codes, and any other legal requirements in your area.

4. Maximizing Efficiency: They optimize your barndominium for natural light, energy efficiency, and effective use of space.

When to Hire an Architect:

If you want a fully customized barndominium or if your design includes complex structural or aesthetic elements, an architect is essential. For simpler builds, pre-designed plans or kits may suffice without requiring an architect's input.

1. Engineers: Ensuring Structural Integrity and Safety

Engineers work closely with architects to ensure that your barndominium is safe, stable, and built to last. While architects focus on design, engineers focus on the technical aspects of construction, ensuring the structure can withstand environmental and load conditions.

Key Responsibilities:

1. Structural Engineering:

Engineers calculate load-bearing requirements, ensuring your foundation, walls, and roof can support the weight of the structure and resist environmental stresses like wind, snow, or earthquakes.

- They address any unique challenges posed by your site, such as uneven terrain or poor soil conditions.

2. Electrical, Plumbing, and HVAC Systems:
Engineers design safe and efficient layouts for

utilities, ensuring proper functionality while meeting building codes.

3. Safety and Compliance: They verify that all structural elements comply with local regulations, ensuring the barndominium is safe for occupancy.

4. Environmental Considerations: Engineers can recommend eco-friendly or energy-efficient options, such as solar panels, geothermal systems, or sustainable materials.

5. When to Hire an Engineer: For any barndominium project involving unique designs, challenging site conditions, or complex utility systems, an engineer's expertise is critical. They're also often required for permits and inspections.

D. Builders: Bringing the Vision to Life

Builders (or general contractors) are the hands-on professionals who manage the physical construction of your barndominium. They bring together materials, tools, and labor to turn your plans into a completed structure.

Key Responsibilities:

1. Construction Management: Builders oversee every stage of construction, from laying the foundation to roofing and finishing.

- They coordinate subcontractors, such as electricians, plumbers, and framers, to ensure the project stays on schedule and within budget.

2. Material Sourcing: Builders often have established relationships with suppliers, which can help secure quality materials at competitive prices.

3. Problem Solving: Experienced builders are skilled at addressing on-site issues, such as weather delays or unexpected design challenges, without compromising quality.

4. Adherence to Plans: Builders ensure the work aligns with architectural and engineering plans, maintaining consistency throughout the project.

When to Hire a Builder:

A builder is essential for anyone not taking a DIY approach. Even if you handle certain parts of the project yourself, hiring a builder for the more technical or labor-intensive aspects (like framing, roofing, or utility installation) is highly recommended.

E. Interior Designers: Perfecting the Look and Feel

While architects and builders focus on the structure, interior designers focus on the look and functionality of your barndominium's interior spaces. They help you choose finishes, furnishings, and layouts that reflect your style and enhance comfort.

Key Responsibilities:

1. Space Planning: Interior designers optimize room layouts to ensure your barndominium feels spacious and functional, even in open-concept designs.

2. Aesthetic Choices: They guide you through selecting materials, colors, and finishes that align with your preferred style—whether rustic, modern, industrial, or a mix.

- They can incorporate design elements like custom lighting, built-ins, or accent walls.

3. Furniture and Décor: Designers assist with choosing furniture and decorative elements that fit the space and reflect your personality.

4. Budget Management: They help you achieve a polished look while staying within your budget, offering cost-effective alternatives where needed.

When to Hire an Interior Designer:

Interior designers are a great addition if you want a cohesive, professional finish to your barndominium or if you're unsure how to balance aesthetics and functionality. If you have a strong design vision and prefer to handle decorating yourself, this role may not be necessary.

How These Professionals Work Together

The collaboration between architects, engineers, builders, and interior designers is critical to the success of your barndominium. Here's how they typically interact:

1. Architects and Engineers: Architects design the vision, and engineers ensure the design is structurally sound and feasible.

2. Builders and Architects/Engineers: Builders bring the plans to life, consulting with architects and engineers to resolve any challenges during construction.

3. Interior Designers and Builders: Designers work with builders to incorporate features like custom cabinetry, lighting, and finishes into the construction process.

This teamwork ensures that all aspects of your barndominium from structure to style are aligned, safe, and cohesive.

Note that each professional architects, engineers, builders, and interior designers plays a unique and essential role in creating a successful barndominium. Architects bring your vision to life, engineers ensure its safety and functionality, builders construct it, and interior designers perfect its look and feel. While hiring these experts adds to the overall cost of your project, their expertise can save time, minimize mistakes, and result in a barndominium that meets your expectations and stands the test of time.

D. Tips for Finding Reliable Contractors and Avoiding Scams

Choosing the right contractor for your barndominium project is a critical step in ensuring a smooth and successful build. Reliable contractors bring expertise, efficiency, and professionalism, while hiring the wrong contractor or falling victim to a scam can lead to costly mistakes, delays, and subpar results. To protect yourself and your investment, follow these tips for finding trustworthy contractors and avoiding potential scams.

1. Do Thorough Research

Before hiring a contractor, invest time in researching potential candidates. Look for contractors with experience in barndominiums or similar construction projects, as this specialization ensures they understand the unique requirements of your build.

- Check Credentials: Verify that the contractor is licensed, bonded, and insured. Licensing requirements vary by state, so confirm their credentials with your local licensing board.
- Review Their Portfolio: Ask for examples of previous projects to assess their experience and quality of work. Pay particular attention to projects similar to yours in size and complexity.
- Read Online Reviews: Look for reviews on platforms like Google, Yelp, or the Better Business Bureau. Pay attention to both positive and negative feedback, and look for patterns in the reviews.
- Ask for Recommendations: Seek referrals from friends, family, or other barndominium owners who have had positive experiences with contractors.

2. Interview Multiple Contractors

Don't settle for the first contractor you find. Interview at least three candidates to compare their qualifications, experience, and pricing.

Ask Detailed Questions:

- How many similar projects have you completed?
- Are you familiar with local zoning laws and building codes?
- Can you provide references from past clients?

a. Gauge Communication Skills: A good contractor should listen to your ideas, address your concerns, and communicate clearly. Poor communication during the interview phase could signal issues later in the project.

b. Visit Active or Completed Sites: If possible, visit one of their active job sites or completed projects to see their work quality and job site management.

3. Verify References

Always ask for and check references from previous clients. A reliable contractor will be happy to provide a list of satisfied customers.

- Contact Past Clients: Ask them about their experience with the contractor, including the quality of work, adherence to timelines, communication, and how they handled issues or changes.
- Look for Consistency: If multiple references mention the same positive (or negative) traits, you'll have a better idea of what to expect.

4. Get Multiple Written Estimates

Request detailed, written estimates from all contractors you're considering. This will help you compare costs, timelines, and the scope of work.

- Be Specific About Your Project: Provide contractors with as much information as possible, including plans, materials, and design preferences. This ensures accurate estimates.
- Watch for Red Flags: Avoid contractors who give vague or overly low estimates. Unrealistically low bids may indicate they'll cut corners, use inferior materials, or tack on hidden costs later.

5. Ensure Contracts Are Detailed and Comprehensive

A professional contractor should provide a written contract that clearly outlines every aspect of the project. Review it carefully before signing.

What to Include in the Contract:

- Scope of work (detailed description of tasks).
- Start and completion dates.

- Payment schedule (e.g., deposit, milestones, final payment).
- Materials and costs.
- Warranties on workmanship and materials.

Avoid Paying Upfront: Reputable contractors typically require a deposit of 10–20% upfront, not full payment. Beware of anyone demanding a large payment before work begins.

6. Verify Insurance and Bonding

Contractors should carry general liability insurance and worker's compensation insurance to protect you in case of accidents or damages during the project.

- Request Proof of Insurance: Ask for copies of their insurance certificates and ensure they're up to date.
- Bonding: A bonded contractor has a guarantee to complete the work as agreed.

This adds another layer of financial protection for you.

7. Avoid High-Pressure Sales Tactics

Be cautious of contractors who use aggressive sales tactics or try to pressure you into making quick decisions. Scammers often use urgency to trick homeowners into signing contracts or making payments without adequate research.

- Take Your Time: A reputable contractor will respect your decision-making process and provide answers to your questions without rushing you.
- Get Everything in Writing: Avoid verbal agreements, as they can lead to disputes later.

8. Beware of Red Flags

Keep an eye out for signs that a contractor may not be trustworthy. Common red flags include:

- Lack of Credentials: They can't provide a license, insurance, or references.
- Cash-Only Payments: They insist on cash payments or refuse to provide receipts.
- No Written Contract: They avoid providing a detailed, written agreement.
- Frequent Excuses or Delays: They fail to show up on time or miss deadlines during initial meetings.
- Overly Low Estimates: Unrealistic pricing could indicate inexperience or an intention to cut corners.

9. Monitor the Work Regularly

Once construction begins, stay involved in the process to ensure the project progresses as planned.

- Inspect the Site: Visit regularly to check the quality of work and confirm it matches the agreed-upon plans.

- Communicate Frequently: Maintain open communication with the contractor to address any questions, changes, or concerns promptly.
- Track Payments: Pay according to the agreed-upon schedule, and only release final payment after all work is completed to your satisfaction.

10. Use a Payment Protection Method

Whenever possible, use payment methods that offer traceability and protection. Avoid paying in cash. Instead, consider the following:

- Checks, credit cards, or bank transfers.
- Escrow accounts, which hold funds until work milestones are completed to your satisfaction.

11. Trust Your Instincts

If something feels off about a contractor whether it's poor communication, reluctance to share credentials, or an unprofessional attitude trust your gut and look for another option. It's better to delay your project to find the right contractor than to rush and hire the wrong one.

Chapter 7

Getting the Permits and Approvals for Your Barndominium

Obtaining the necessary permits and approvals is one of the most important steps in building your barndominium. This process ensures your project complies with local laws, building codes, and safety regulations, helping you avoid legal or financial complications down the road. While navigating the permit process can feel daunting, understanding the requirements and steps involved will make it much easier to manage. Here's a comprehensive guide to help you get the permits and approvals needed for your barndominium.

A. How to Navigate Local Building Regulations for Your Barndominium

Understanding and navigating local building regulations is a critical step in constructing your barndominium. Building regulations, also known as building codes, zoning laws, and permitting requirements, ensure that your project is safe, structurally sound, and compliant with local laws. Although regulations can seem complex, breaking the process down into manageable steps can make it much easier to navigate and avoid costly mistakes. Here's a step-by-step guide to help you understand and work with local building regulations.

Step 1: Research Local Zoning Laws

Zoning laws govern how a piece of land can be used, and they vary widely depending on your location. These regulations specify whether your land is zoned for residential, agricultural, commercial, or mixed use.

What to Do:

- Contact your local zoning office or planning department to confirm how your property is zoned.

- Ensure that building a barndominium aligns with the zoning designation. For example:
- Agricultural zones may allow barndominiums, but you might need to meet specific requirements if the property will house livestock.
- Residential zones may require certain aesthetic or structural elements to match neighborhood standards.

Check for restrictions like:

- Setback Requirements: Distance your structure must be from property lines, roads, or neighboring buildings.
- Height Limits: Maximum allowable height for structures in your area.
- Lot Coverage: Percentage of land your building can occupy.
- Easements: Areas where construction is restricted due to utilities, shared access, or environmental concerns.

Step 2: Understand Building Codes

Building codes are detailed regulations that govern the design, construction, and safety of your structure. These are designed to protect occupants and ensure long-term structural integrity.

What to Do:

Obtain a copy of your local building codes from the building department or state code authority.

Review the codes for requirements specific to:

- Foundations: Soil testing may be required to ensure the ground is stable enough to support your barndominium.
- Framing and Structural Integrity: Minimum load-bearing requirements to withstand wind, snow, or earthquakes.
- Roofing: Fire resistance, slope, and material standards.

- Electrical and Plumbing: Requirements for wiring, outlets, water pressure, and pipe materials.
- Energy Efficiency: Insulation, window, and HVAC standards for energy compliance.

Note: Consult professionals like engineers or builders to interpret technical aspects of the codes if necessary.

Step 3: Identify Permit Requirements

Most municipalities require permits before construction can begin. These permits ensure that your project complies with zoning laws and building codes.

What to Do:

Visit your local permit office or municipal website to determine which permits you'll need. Common permits include:

- Building permit.
- Electrical, plumbing, and HVAC permits.

- Environmental permits (for areas near wetlands, rivers, or protected land).
- Driveway or septic system permits.
- Submit detailed plans and documents, including:
- Site plans.
- Structural blueprints.
- Engineering calculations.
- Proof of property ownership.

Pay permit fees and wait for approval before starting construction.

Step 4: Address Environmental Regulations

If your property is in a rural or environmentally sensitive area, additional regulations may apply to protect the surrounding ecosystem.

What to Do:

Check if your property falls within a floodplain, wetland, or protected wildlife zone.

Obtain clearance from agencies like the Environmental Protection Agency (EPA) or local environmental boards, if applicable.

Plan for mitigation measures, such as:

- Elevating the foundation in flood-prone areas.
- Managing stormwater runoff.
- Following restrictions on tree removal or land grading.

Step 5: Work with Professionals

Professionals such as architects, engineers, and contractors are often familiar with local building regulations and can guide you through the process.

What to Do:

- Hire an Architect or Engineer: They can design your barndominium to meet structural and zoning requirements.
- Consult with Contractors: Many contractors have experience navigating local regulations

and can manage permits and inspections for you.

- Seek Local Expertise: Professionals familiar with your area's codes can help prevent delays caused by compliance issues.

Step 6: Prepare for Inspections

During construction, inspectors will visit your site to ensure the project meets building codes and the approved plans. Passing inspections is crucial to avoid fines or project delays.

What to Do:

Schedule inspections at key stages, such as:

- After the foundation is poured.
- During framing, plumbing, and electrical work.
- At project completion for the final inspection.
- Be prepared to make adjustments if the inspector identifies any issues.

- Keep detailed records of all inspections and approvals.

Step 7: Stay Updated on Regulations

Building regulations can change over time, so it's important to stay informed throughout your project.

What to Do:

- Regularly check with local authorities for updates or amendments to codes or zoning laws.
- Communicate with your builder or project manager to ensure compliance with any changes.

Tips for Navigating Local Building Regulations

1. Start Early: Begin researching regulations before purchasing land or finalizing your design.

2. Be Organized: Keep all plans, permits, and correspondence with regulatory authorities in one place.

3. Ask Questions: Don't hesitate to ask local officials or professionals for clarification if something is unclear.

4. Budget for Permits and Fees: Include permitting costs in your overall project budget to avoid surprises.

5. Work with the Right Professionals: Architects, engineers, and contractors familiar with your area's requirements can save you time and stress.

6. Avoid Cutting Corners: Failing to comply with regulations can result in fines, delays, or even having to tear down parts of your build.

Common Challenges and How to Overcome Them

Challenge: Navigating complex zoning laws.

Solution: Work with a local zoning consultant or architect familiar with your area's requirements.

Challenge: Delays in permit approvals.

Solution: Submit complete and accurate plans upfront and respond promptly to any requests for additional information.

Challenge: Conflicts with neighbors or community boards.

Solution: Engage in open communication and address concerns before construction begins.

Navigating local building regulations is a necessary but manageable part of building your barndominium. By thoroughly researching zoning laws, building codes, and permit requirements, you can ensure your project proceeds smoothly and legally. Working with experienced professionals, staying organized, and addressing potential challenges proactively will help you avoid delays and costly mistakes.

B. Common Permits You'll Need to Build a Barndominium

Before starting construction on your barndominium, it's essential to obtain the necessary permits. These permits ensure your project complies with local laws, building codes, and safety regulations, protecting both your investment and your future home. Here's a breakdown of the most common permits you'll need to secure for your barndominium project:

1. Zoning Permit

Purpose: Ensures your property is zoned for the type of structure you're building and its intended use.

What It Covers:

- Residential, agricultural, or mixed-use zoning compliance.
- Setbacks (distance from property lines or other structures).

- Height and size restrictions.
- Easements (areas reserved for utilities or shared access).

When It's Required: Before you begin any construction, including site preparation.

2. Building Permit

Purpose: The main permit required for construction, ensuring your barndominium meets local building codes and safety standards.

What It Covers:

- Structural design and integrity (foundation, walls, framing, roof).
- Compliance with fire safety, wind, and earthquake standards.
- Overall layout and size.

When It's Required: Before beginning any physical construction work.

3. Foundation Permit

Purpose: Ensures the foundation is properly designed and installed to support the structure.

What It Covers:

- Soil testing and grading (to ensure the ground is stable).
- Footings, slab thickness, or piers.
- Reinforcement requirements (e.g., rebar).

When It's Required: Before pouring concrete or laying any foundation materials.

4. Electrical Permit

Purpose: Regulates the installation of electrical systems to ensure safety and code compliance.

What It Covers:

- Wiring, outlets, and circuit breaker installations.
- Light fixtures, ceiling fans, and other electrical components.

- Renewable energy systems, such as solar panels.

When It's Required: Before starting any electrical work, often inspected at different stages of installation.

5. Plumbing Permit

Purpose: Oversees the installation of plumbing systems, ensuring proper function and safety.

What It Covers:

- Water lines, sinks, showers, and toilets.
- Sewer connections or septic systems.
- Water heaters and drainage systems.

When It's Required: Before installing any plumbing systems, often with multiple inspections (rough-in and final).

6. HVAC Permit

Purpose: Ensures the heating, ventilation, and air conditioning systems are installed correctly and meet energy efficiency standards.

What It Covers:

- Ductwork, air conditioning units, and furnaces.
- Ventilation systems for kitchens and bathrooms.
- Energy-efficient upgrades, such as heat pumps or geothermal systems.

When It's Required: Before installing any HVAC equipment.

7. Septic System Permit (If Needed)

Purpose: Required if your property is not connected to a municipal sewer system and you need to install a septic tank.

What It Covers:

- Site evaluation for soil permeability.
- Design and location of the septic tank and drain field.
- Inspections for proper installation.

When It's Required: Before breaking ground for a septic system.

8. Well Permit (If Needed)

Purpose: Required if your property needs a private well for water.

What It Covers:

- Drilling and placement of the well.
- Water quality testing to ensure it's safe for drinking.
- Pump installation and maintenance requirements.

When It's Required: Before drilling begins.

9. Environmental Permits

Purpose: Protects environmentally sensitive areas and ensures minimal impact on the surrounding ecosystem.

What It Covers:

- Construction near wetlands, rivers, or other protected areas.
- Managing stormwater runoff and drainage.
- Erosion control during construction.

When It's Required: If your property is in or near environmentally sensitive areas, consult local environmental agencies.

10. Driveway Permit

Purpose: Regulates the construction of driveways or access roads connecting your property to public roads.

What It Covers:

- Placement and dimensions of the driveway.

- Compliance with road safety standards.
- Drainage systems around the driveway.

When It's Required: Before creating or modifying a driveway.

11. Demolition Permit (If Needed)

Purpose: Required if you need to remove existing structures on your property before starting construction.

What It Covers:

- Safe removal of structures like barns, sheds, or old homes.
- Disposal of materials and handling of hazardous substances (e.g., asbestos).

When It's Required: Before demolishing any structures.

12. Occupancy Permit

Purpose: The final permit that certifies your barndominium is safe for living.

What It Covers:

- Completion of all construction and systems (electrical, plumbing, HVAC).
- Compliance with approved plans and building codes.

When It's Required: After all inspections are complete and before you move in.

How to Secure Permits

1. Contact Local Authorities: Start by visiting your city or county building department to obtain a list of required permits and applications.

2. Prepare Documents: Submit detailed plans, including blueprints, site maps, and engineering calculations, if needed.

3. Pay Fees: Permitting fees vary by location and scope of the project, so budget accordingly.

4. Schedule Inspections: Be prepared for inspections at various stages of construction to ensure compliance.

5. Work with Professionals: Architects, engineers, or contractors can help navigate the permitting process and ensure your plans meet local regulations.

Securing the necessary permits is a vital step in building your barndominium. By understanding the specific permits you'll need uch as zoning, building, plumbing, and electrical you can avoid delays, fines, and compliance issues.

C. How to Avoid Delays in the Approval Process

Delays in the approval process for building permits can derail your barndominium project, costing time and money. To keep your project on schedule, you must approach the permitting process with thorough preparation and attention to detail.

1. The first step to avoiding delays is "researching local regulations early". Contact your local building department to understand the specific permits you'll need for zoning, construction, and utilities. Familiarize yourself with requirements such as setbacks, height limits, and environmental regulations. Ensuring your plans align with these rules will prevent your application from being rejected or sent back for revisions.

2. Submitting a complete and accurate application is critical. Missing documents, vague blueprints, or incomplete site plans are common reasons for delays. Work with architects or engineers to prepare detailed and professional plans, as this can expedite the review process. Include all necessary documentation, such as site surveys, structural calculations, and proof of ownership.

3. Be proactive in communication. Stay in touch with permitting officials throughout the review process and respond promptly to any requests for

additional information or changes. Delays often occur when applicants fail to address issues in a timely manner.

4. Budget for inspections and revisions. Many approvals require multiple inspections during construction. Scheduling these in advance and ensuring your site is ready for inspection can help you avoid bottlenecks.

Lastly, consider hiring professionals, such as contractors or permitting consultants, who are familiar with local requirements. Their expertise can prevent costly mistakes and ensure your plans meet code the first time.

Chapter 8

Choosing Materials and Construction Options for Your Barndominium

Selecting the right materials and construction methods for your barndominium is a critical step that affects its durability, aesthetics, energy efficiency, and overall cost. Your choices should align with your budget, design goals, and the climate and environmental conditions of your location. Below is a guide to help you with these decisions and make informed choices for your barndominium project.

1. Structural Materials: Metal vs. Wood

The two primary structural materials for barndominiums are "metal and wood". Each has its advantages and considerations:

1. Metal Frames

Benefits:

- Highly durable and resistant to pests, fire, and extreme weather.
- Low maintenance compared to wood.
- Offers a modern, industrial aesthetic.
- Allows for open floor plans due to fewer load-bearing walls.

Considerations:

- Can be more expensive initially.
- Requires proper insulation to manage temperature and prevent condensation in certain climates.

2. Wood Frames

Benefits:

- Provides a more traditional, rustic look.
- Easier for DIY builders or small-scale contractors to work with.
- Typically less expensive upfront.

Considerations:

- More prone to pests (e.g., termites) and fire.
- Requires regular maintenance, such as sealing or staining, to prevent rot or warping.

3. Exterior Siding Options

Your choice of exterior siding impacts both the appearance and durability of your barndominium. Popular options include:

1. Metal Siding

- Pros: Long-lasting, low maintenance, resistant to weather and pests.
- Cons: Can dent from impacts and may not fit all aesthetic preferences.

2. Wood Siding

- Pros: Offers a natural, warm look that suits rural or rustic styles.

- Cons: Requires regular maintenance and is susceptible to rot and pests.

3. Fiber Cement Siding

- Pros: Highly durable, fire-resistant, and available in various textures and colors.
- Cons: Higher installation cost and more brittle than other materials.

4. Brick or Stone Veneer

- Pros: Enhances curb appeal with a classic, upscale look.
- Cons: Expensive and adds significant weight to the structure.

4. Roofing Options

The roof of your barndominium should combine durability, energy efficiency, and aesthetics. Common options include:

1. Metal Roofing

- Pros: Long lifespan (40+ years), lightweight, and energy-efficient.
- Cons: Can be noisy during heavy rain or hail without proper insulation.

2. Asphalt Shingles

- Pros: Affordable and available in various colors and styles.
- Cons: Shorter lifespan (20–30 years) and requires more frequent maintenance.

3. Clay or Concrete Tiles

- Pros: Excellent for hot climates due to their heat resistance.
- Cons: Heavy and expensive to install.

5. Insulation Options

Insulation is essential for maintaining comfortable temperatures and improving energy efficiency. The right insulation depends on your climate and budget.

1. Spray Foam Insulation

- Pros: Provides excellent thermal resistance and seals gaps to prevent air leaks.
- Cons: Higher upfront cost.

2. Fiberglass Insulation

- Pros: Affordable and widely available.
- Cons: Less effective at sealing air leaks and prone to moisture absorption.

3. Rigid Foam Panels

- Pros: Durable, moisture-resistant, and great for insulating walls and roofs.
- Cons: More expensive and harder to install in irregular spaces.

4. Reflective or Radiant Barriers

- Pros: Ideal for hot climates to reduce heat gain.
- Cons: Less effective in cold climates.

6. Flooring Options

Your flooring choice should reflect the intended use of your barndominium, as well as your budget and style preferences.

1. Concrete Floors

- Pros: Durable, low-maintenance, and can be polished or stained for a modern look.
- Cons: Can feel cold and hard underfoot without proper insulation or rugs.

2. Hardwood or Engineered Wood

- Pros: Warm, classic look that adds value to your home.
- Cons: Expensive and susceptible to moisture damage.

3. Vinyl or Laminate Flooring

- Pros: Affordable, water-resistant, and available in a variety of styles.

- Cons: Less durable than other options and may feel less premium.

4. Tile Flooring

- Pros: Great for kitchens and bathrooms due to water resistance.
- Cons: Can be expensive and cold without radiant heating.

2. Windows and Doors

Windows and doors play a key role in energy efficiency, security, and overall design.

- Energy Efficient Windows: Look for double or triple pane windows with low-E coatings to reduce heat transfer.
- Doors: Steel or fiberglass doors offer durability and insulation, while wood doors provide a timeless aesthetic.
- Sliding or French Doors: Consider large glass doors to enhance natural light and

create a connection between indoor and outdoor spaces.

3. Pre-Fabricated Kits vs. Custom Builds

When choosing construction options, you'll need to decide between pre-fabricated kits and fully custom builds.

Pre-Fabricated Kits

Pros:

- Faster to assemble, often saving time and labor costs.
- Easier for DIY builders with limited experience.
- Often includes structural components like framing, siding, and roofing.

Cons:

- Limited customization options.
- May require modifications to fit your specific needs.

Custom Builds

Pros:

- Allows complete freedom in design and materials.
- Ideal for unique layouts or features (e.g., workshops, lofts, or hybrid spaces).

Cons:

- More expensive and time-intensive.
- Requires experienced professionals for design and construction.

4. Sustainability and Energy Efficiency

If eco-friendliness is a priority, consider sustainable materials and energy-efficient upgrades:

- Solar Panels: Reduce energy costs and reliance on the grid.

- Recycled Materials: Use reclaimed wood, steel, or other recycled materials for flooring, siding, or finishes.
- Energy Star Appliances: Lower your long-term utility costs with efficient appliances.

Choosing the right materials and construction options for your barndominium requires balancing durability, aesthetics, and budget. By considering factors such as structural materials, siding, roofing, insulation, and energy efficiency, you can create a home that meets your needs and lasts for years to come.

Chapter 9

The Construction Process for Your Barndominium

Building a barndominium is an exciting and rewarding process, but it requires careful planning, organization, and execution. Understanding each phase of construction will help you manage the project effectively, whether you're taking a DIY approach or working with contractors.

Here's an overview of the typical construction process for a barndominium, from site preparation to finishing touches.

A. Breaking Ground: Site Preparation and Laying the Foundation

The site preparation and foundation stages are among the most critical parts of the construction process for your barndominium. These steps ensure that the land is stable and ready to support the structure, setting the stage for a successful build. Proper planning and execution during this phase can prevent costly issues later in the project.

1. Site Preparation

Site preparation involves clearing and preparing the land to create a solid, level surface for the foundation.

1. Land Clearing

- Remove Obstacles: Trees, bushes, rocks, and other debris must be cleared from the building site. This ensures a safe, accessible workspace and prevents structural issues caused by root systems or uneven terrain.

- Grading and Leveling: The land must be leveled to create a stable base. Grading also helps with water drainage, reducing the risk of water pooling around or under the foundation.
- Drainage Planning: Incorporate sloping or drainage systems to channel water away from the building site, particularly in areas prone to heavy rainfall.

2. Soil Testing

Why It's Important: The strength and composition of the soil affect the type of foundation required. Poor soil conditions can lead to settling or structural instability.

- Testing Process: A professional geotechnical engineer can perform soil tests to assess load-bearing capacity, moisture content, and drainage characteristics.

- Soil Stabilization: If the soil is not ideal, techniques like compacting, adding gravel, or mixing in stabilizing agents may be necessary.

3. Utility Planning

- Water and Sewer Connections: Determine whether your property will connect to municipal systems or require a septic system and well.

- Electricity and Gas: Arrange for utility hookups or plan for alternatives like solar power or propane tanks.

- Underground Lines: Check for existing underground lines using local utility services to avoid damaging them during construction.

4. Permits and Approvals

Secure all necessary permits before breaking ground. These may include zoning, environmental, and building permits specific to your area.

2. Laying the Foundation

The foundation is essential to the structural integrity of your barndominium. It supports the weight of the structure and distributes it evenly across the ground, preventing settling or shifting over time.

1. Choose the Right Foundation Type

The type of foundation you need depends on your design, soil conditions, and budget.

a. Concrete Slab Foundation: The concrete slab foundation is the most common for barndominiums.

- A flat, continuous layer of concrete that supports the entire structure.
- Ideal for areas with stable soil and minimal frost.

b. Pier-and-Beam Foundation:

- Consists of piers sunk into the ground to support beams and the structure above.
- Useful in areas with poor soil or where elevation is needed for flood protection.

c. Crawlspace Foundation:

- Raises the structure slightly off the ground, creating a small space beneath the floor.
- Provides better access to plumbing and electrical systems.

2. Excavation and Preparation

- Mark the Site: Use stakes, flags, or string to outline the foundation's exact dimensions according to your blueprints.
- Excavate: Remove soil to the required depth based on the foundation type and building plans.

- Add a Gravel Base: Spread a layer of gravel to improve drainage and create a stable base for the concrete.

3. Reinforce the Foundation

- Install Rebar: Reinforcing steel bars (rebar) are added to the foundation to provide additional strength and reduce cracking.
- Formwork: Wooden or metal forms are built around the perimeter of the foundation to hold the concrete in place as it sets.

4. Pouring the Concrete

- Mix and Pour: Concrete is mixed and poured into the forms. For large foundations, ready-mix concrete trucks may be used to ensure consistency.
- Level the Surface: Use a screed or similar tool to smooth the surface and remove air pockets.

- Curing: Allow the concrete to cure for several days. Proper curing is essential to achieve the desired strength and durability.

5. Inspection

Before proceeding with construction, schedule an inspection to ensure the foundation meets local building codes and project specifications.

Tips for Success

1. Plan Ahead: Address drainage, utilities, and soil testing early to avoid delays.
2. Hire Professionals: For complex tasks like soil testing and foundation pouring, consider hiring experienced contractors.
3. Weather Considerations: Avoid pouring concrete during extreme weather conditions, as temperature and moisture can affect curing.
4. Double-Check Measurements: Ensure the foundation aligns perfectly with your

building plans to avoid complications during framing.

Note that breaking ground and laying the foundation are the first major steps in building your barndominium. By preparing the site carefully, selecting the right foundation type, and ensuring compliance with local regulations, you'll create a stable base for a strong and durable structure.

B. Step-by-Step Breakdown of the Barndominium Building Process

Building a barndominium involves several key stages, from framing the structure to installing utilities and finishing the interior. Each step requires careful planning and execution to ensure your project is structurally sound, functional, and aligned with your vision. Here's a detailed step-by-step guide to help you understand the process.

1. Framing the Structure

Framing is the skeleton of your barndominium and provides the shape and structural integrity of the building.

a. Metal or Wood Frame Construction: Most barndominiums use steel frames for durability and open floor plans, though wood is an option for those seeking a more traditional aesthetic.

- Prefabricated metal frame kits are common and allow for faster assembly.

b. Assembling the Frame: Begin by erecting vertical columns or posts, ensuring they're properly anchored to the foundation.

- Connect horizontal beams to the columns to form the basic structure. Add roof trusses or rafters, ensuring proper alignment and stability.

c. Bracing and Securing: Install temporary bracing during assembly to prevent movement.

- Tighten bolts and fasteners securely for stability.

2. Installing Exterior Walls

Exterior walls protect your barndominium from the elements and define its aesthetic.

a. Metal Siding Installation: Attach prefabricated metal panels to the frame using screws or bolts. Overlapping panels provide water resistance.

- Add corner trim and flashing for a finished look and to prevent leaks.

b. Wood or Alternative Siding: If you opt for wood, fiber cement, or stone veneer siding, install it according to the manufacturer's instructions.

- Ensure proper sealing and weatherproofing to prevent rot or water damage.

c. Adding Insulation: Insulate the walls during or after exterior wall installation using spray foam, fiberglass, or rigid foam insulation.

3. Roofing Installation

The roof protects your barndominium from weather and contributes to its overall structural strength.

a. Metal Roof Panels: Attach metal roofing panels to the trusses using screws with rubber washers for a watertight seal.

- Overlap panels to ensure water runoff and prevent leaks.

b. Ventilation and Insulation: Install ridge vents, soffit vents, or other ventilation systems to regulate airflow and prevent moisture buildup.

- Add insulation under the roof to maintain energy efficiency.

c. Gutters and Downspouts: Install a gutter system to direct rainwater away from the foundation.

4. Installing Windows and Doors

Windows and doors provide functionality, natural light, and ventilation while enhancing the building's design.

a. Window Installation:

- Place windows into pre-cut openings, ensuring a snug fit.
- Seal edges with weatherproof caulking or flashing to prevent leaks.

b. Door Installation:

- Hang exterior doors securely with weatherstripping to improve energy efficiency.
- Sliding barn doors, French doors, or traditional entry doors are popular choices for barndominiums.

5. Plumbing and Electrical Systems

These utilities are crucial for making your barndominium functional and livable.

1. Plumbing;

Install Water Lines and Drains:

- Lay pipes for water supply and drainage according to your floor plan.
- Connect plumbing to a septic system or municipal sewage system.

Water Fixtures:

- Rough-in locations for sinks, showers, toilets, and water heaters.
- Install pipes before covering walls to allow for inspections.

2. Electrical Wiring;

Run Electrical Lines:

- Install wiring for outlets, switches, and light fixtures within the walls and ceilings.

- Follow local electrical codes to ensure safety and compliance.

Install the Electrical Panel:

- Mount the breaker box and connect it to the main power supply.
- Label circuits for easy identification.

Plan for Smart Systems: Add wiring for security systems, internet, or smart home features during this phase.

6. HVAC Installation

Heating, ventilation, and air conditioning systems ensure your barndominium is comfortable year-round.

a. Ductwork Installation: If using a central HVAC system, install ductwork within the walls and ceilings.

- Ensure proper sealing to prevent energy loss.

b. Unit Installation: Place the furnace, air conditioning unit, or heat pump in the designated location.

- Connect the HVAC system to the electrical and plumbing systems.

7. Insulating the Interior

Proper insulation improves energy efficiency and comfort.

a. Spray Foam Insulation: Ideal for metal-framed barndominiums because it seals gaps and reduces condensation.

b. Fiberglass or Rigid Foam: Common in walls, floors, and ceilings to regulate temperature and noise.

c. Radiant Barriers: Useful under the roof to reflect heat in warm climates.

8. Interior Walls and Ceilings

The interior walls and ceilings define the spaces within your barndominium and complete the structure.

a. Framing Interior Walls: Use wood or metal studs to frame walls based on your floor plan.

- Installing Drywall or Paneling:
- Hang drywall or wood paneling, then tape, sand, and finish seams.
- Consider adding texture or paint for the desired look.

b. Ceilings: Install ceiling panels, drywall, or exposed beams, depending on your design style.

9. Flooring Installation

Flooring provides both function and style and is typically installed toward the end of construction.

a. Concrete Floors: Polish or stain concrete floors for a modern, durable finish.

Wood, Vinyl, or Laminate: Install planks or tiles, ensuring proper alignment and sealing.

b. Tile Flooring: Ideal for kitchens, bathrooms, or utility spaces.

10. Finishing Touches

The final stage of construction brings everything together and personalizes the space.

a. Painting and Trim: Paint walls and ceilings in your chosen colors.

- Add baseboards, crown molding, and trim around windows and doors.

b. Lighting and Fixtures: Install light fixtures, ceiling fans, and other decorative elements.

c. Cabinetry and Appliances: Add cabinets, countertops, and appliances in the kitchen and bathrooms.

d. Decorative Features: Incorporate design elements such as barn doors, accent walls, or custom shelving to complete the look.

11. Final Inspections and Occupancy

Before moving in, your barndominium must pass final inspections to ensure everything is safe and up to code.

- Schedule Inspections: Local authorities will inspect plumbing, electrical, HVAC, and structural elements.
- Obtain the Certificate of Occupancy: Once the inspections are complete, you'll receive approval to move in.

The barndominium construction process involves several interconnected steps, from framing and utilities to finishing the interior. Whether you're building it yourself or working with contractors, understanding these stages will help you manage the project effectively and ensure your barndominium is safe, functional, and beautifully designed.

C. Working with Contractors to Stay on Schedule

Managing a construction project like a barndominium requires coordination with contractors to ensure the project stays on schedule. Delays can lead to increased costs, stress, and complications, so proactive communication and planning are essential to keeping everything on track. Here are actionable strategies to help you work effectively with contractors and ensure timely completion of your barndominium.

1. Choose Reliable Contractors

The first step in staying on schedule is hiring experienced, trustworthy contractors who have a proven track record of completing projects on time.

- Research and References: Choose contractors with solid reviews, verifiable references, and experience in barndominium construction.
- Check Licensing and Insurance: Verify credentials to avoid delays caused by improper work or legal complications.

2. Establish a Detailed Timeline

A clear and realistic timeline is the foundation of a smooth project.

- Create a Construction Schedule: Work with your contractor to outline each phase of the project, from site preparation to finishing touches. Include deadlines for tasks like framing, roofing, plumbing, and inspections.
- Identify Milestones: Break the project into manageable parts with specific milestones, such as completing the foundation or installing the roof. This helps track progress and identify potential delays early.

- Account for Contingencies: Build in buffer time for weather, material delays, or unexpected challenges to avoid major disruptions.

3. Maintain Open Communication

Consistent communication is key to keeping your contractors aligned with your expectations.

- Schedule Regular Check-Ins: Set up weekly or bi-weekly meetings to review progress, address issues, and adjust timelines if necessary.
- Use Technology: Project management apps like Buildertrend, CoConstruct, or simple spreadsheets can help you track progress and share updates with contractors.
- Be Available: Make yourself accessible for quick decisions or approvals to avoid holding up work.

4. Provide Clear Expectations

Clarity in your requirements prevents misunderstandings that can lead to delays.

- Detailed Contract: Ensure the contract includes a comprehensive scope of work, the agreed timeline, payment schedule, and responsibilities.
- Written Changes: Document any changes to the project, including timeline adjustments, to avoid disputes or confusion.
- Material Selection: Choose materials early and provide specifications to avoid delays caused by late orders or miscommunications.

5. Monitor Progress Regularly

While it's important to trust your contractors, staying actively involved ensures the project stays on course.

- Visit the Site: Regularly inspect the work to verify it aligns with the timeline and quality expectations.
- Review Milestones: Compare progress against the agreed schedule to catch delays before they escalate.
- Ask Questions: Don't hesitate to ask about potential bottlenecks or challenges to address them proactively.

6. Address Delays Promptly

Delays can happen, but addressing them quickly minimizes their impact.

- Identify the Cause: Determine whether delays are due to weather, materials, or other factors.
- Adjust the Timeline: Work with contractors to create a revised plan that accommodates the delay while keeping the project moving forward.

- Hold Accountability: If the delay is due to the contractor's error, discuss solutions and how they plan to prevent future issues.

7. Align Payments with Progress

Linking payments to milestones ensures contractors remain motivated to stay on schedule.

Progress-Based Payments: Pay contractors as they complete specific stages of the project, such as finishing the foundation or framing.

Retain Final Payment: Hold back a portion of the payment until all work is completed and meets your expectations.

8. Minimize Changes During Construction

Frequent changes to the plan can disrupt schedules and increase costs.

- Finalize Designs Early: Confirm your floor plan, materials, and finishes before construction begins.

- Avoid Mid-Project Changes: Significant design or material changes during construction can cause delays. If changes are necessary, communicate them clearly and document the updated schedule.

9. Account for Inspections

Inspections are required at various stages of construction, and missing one can halt progress.

- Schedule Inspections Early: Work with contractors to plan inspections at the right times (e.g., after pouring the foundation or installing plumbing).
- Prepare for Re-Inspections: If an issue arises during an inspection, resolve it quickly to avoid delays.

10. Foster a Positive Relationship

Building a good rapport with your contractors can lead to smoother communication and better collaboration.

- Be Respectful: Treat contractors professionally and with respect, acknowledging their expertise.
- Offer Feedback: Provide constructive feedback if something isn't meeting your expectations.
- Recognize Good Work: Acknowledging progress and quality work can boost morale and encourage contractors to stay on track.

D. Avoiding Common Construction Pitfalls When Building Your Barndominium

Building a barndominium can be a rewarding process, but without proper planning and oversight, it's easy to encounter common construction pitfalls that can cause delays, increase costs, or compromise the final result. By identifying potential issues ahead of time and addressing them proactively, you can ensure a smoother and more successful construction experience.

1. Inadequate Planning and Design

The Pitfall: Rushing into construction without a detailed plan or clear design often leads to unexpected changes, delays, and cost overruns.

How to Avoid It:

- Work with experienced professionals (architects, engineers, or contractors) to create comprehensive blueprints and plans.
- Finalize your design, layout, and materials before breaking ground.
- Double-check that your plans comply with local building codes and zoning regulations.

2. Budget Mismanagement

The Pitfall: Underestimating costs or failing to account for unexpected expenses can lead to financial strain and incomplete projects.

How to Avoid It:

- Set a realistic budget that includes a 10–20% contingency for unforeseen expenses.
- Get multiple quotes from contractors and suppliers to compare costs.
- Track spending throughout the project to ensure you stay within your budget.

3. Skipping Soil Testing

The Pitfall: Building on unstable soil can result in foundation issues, structural damage, or costly repairs.

How to Avoid It:

- Conduct a professional soil test before site preparation to determine the soil's load-bearing capacity and drainage characteristics.
- Address any soil issues through stabilization, grading, or proper foundation design.

4. Ignoring Building Codes and Permits

The Pitfall: Failing to obtain the necessary permits or meet building codes can lead to fines, delays, or even demolition of unauthorized work.

How to Avoid It:

- Research local building codes and permit requirements early in the planning process.
- Secure all necessary permits before starting construction.
- Schedule inspections as required to ensure compliance at every stage of the project.

5. Poor Contractor Selection

The Pitfall: Hiring inexperienced or unreliable contractors can lead to low-quality work, delays, or disputes.

How to Avoid It:

- Vet contractors thoroughly by checking references, reviews, and credentials.

- Choose contractors with specific experience in barndominium construction.
- Have a detailed contract in place that outlines responsibilities, timelines, and payment terms.

6. Cutting Corners on Materials

The Pitfall: Using cheap or low-quality materials to save money can result in higher maintenance costs, poor durability, and a shorter lifespan for your barndominium.

How to Avoid It:

- Invest in high-quality materials that are suited to your climate and intended use.
- Work with contractors or suppliers to find cost-effective options without sacrificing quality.
- Prioritize durability for key components like the foundation, frame, roof, and insulation.

7. Poor Communication

The Pitfall: Miscommunication with contractors, suppliers, or inspectors can lead to misunderstandings, delays, and mistakes.

How to Avoid It:

- Maintain regular communication with your contractors through weekly check-ins or progress meetings.
- Use project management tools to track schedules, tasks, and updates.
- Document all changes and decisions in writing to avoid disputes.

8. Underestimating Weather Impacts

The Pitfall: Poor weather can delay construction and damage materials if proper precautions aren't taken.

How to Avoid It:

- Plan your construction timeline around seasonal weather patterns, avoiding extreme conditions.
- Protect materials from rain, wind, or extreme temperatures by storing them in covered areas.
- Build in buffer time for weather-related delays in your project schedule.

9. Skipping Inspections

The Pitfall: Failing to schedule required inspections can result in construction errors, legal issues, or project delays.

How to Avoid It:

- Schedule inspections at key milestones, such as after the foundation is poured or electrical and plumbing work is completed.
- Address any issues identified by inspectors promptly to avoid re-inspections or delays.

10. Overlooking Energy Efficiency

The Pitfall: Neglecting energy-efficient design and materials can result in higher utility bills and lower resale value.

How to Avoid It:

- Use proper insulation, energy-efficient windows, and doors to regulate temperature.
- Consider installing energy-efficient HVAC systems, lighting, and appliances.
- Plan for renewable energy options like solar panels, especially in areas with high energy costs.

11. Failing to Plan for Utilities

The Pitfall: Improper planning for water, electrical, and sewage connections can lead to costly modifications or delays.

How to Avoid It:

- Design your utility layouts (plumbing, electrical, and HVAC) early in the process.
- Ensure access to municipal services or plan for alternatives like septic systems or wells.
- Work with licensed professionals to install and inspect utility systems.

12. Neglecting Future Needs

The Pitfall: Designing your barndominium without considering future needs can limit its functionality or require costly renovations later.

How to Avoid It:

- Plan for potential future expansions, such as additional rooms, storage areas, or workshops.
- Include flexible spaces that can serve multiple purposes as your needs change.
- Consider long-term maintenance requirements and durability when choosing materials and systems.

13. Improper Sequencing of Construction Phases

The Pitfall: Starting tasks out of order can lead to inefficiencies, rework, and delays.

How to Avoid It:

- Follow a logical sequence: site preparation → foundation → framing → utilities → interior finishes.
- Coordinate with contractors to ensure tasks are scheduled in the correct order.
- Avoid starting interior work (e.g., drywall) until exterior work is weatherproofed.

Avoiding construction pitfalls requires careful planning, attention to detail, and proactive management. By working with experienced professionals, maintaining open communication, and addressing challenges early, you can ensure your barndominium project stays on track and delivers the durable, functional home you envision.

Chapter 10

Interior Design and Layout for Your Barndominium

The interior design and layout of your barndominium are crucial for creating a functional, comfortable, and visually appealing living space. Barndominiums offer versatility in design, with their open floor plans and customizable layouts, making it possible to reflect your personal style while ensuring practicality. Below is a guide to planning your barndominium's interior design and layout effectively.

1. Start with a Functional Layout

The foundation of great interior design is a layout that fits your lifestyle. Barndominiums are often designed with open floor plans, which allow for flexibility in how spaces are used.

  i. Define Zones: Divide your barndominium into functional zones—living, dining, kitchen, bedrooms, bathrooms, and work or storage spaces.

ii. Maximize Flow: Ensure easy movement between high-traffic areas, like the kitchen, living room, and dining space.

iii. Consider Multi-Use Spaces: Incorporate dual-purpose areas, such as a home office in a loft or a combined living and dining area.

iv. Include Storage: Plan for ample storage, such as walk-in closets, built-in cabinets, or under-stair storage, to maintain a clutter-free environment.

2. Highlight Open-Concept Living

One of the defining features of a barndominium is the open-concept layout. Use this to your advantage to create a spacious and inviting environment.

i. Unify with Flooring: Use the same flooring material throughout the main living areas to create a seamless flow between spaces.

ii. Strategic Furniture Placement: Use furniture, rugs, or room dividers to visually separate spaces without disrupting the open feel.

iii. Vaulted Ceilings: Expose the ceiling trusses or beams to enhance the sense of height and openness.

3. Incorporate Natural Light

Barndominiums typically feature large windows and open spaces, making them ideal for incorporating natural light.

i. Install Oversized Windows: Use floor-to-ceiling windows or sliding glass doors to bring in light and connect indoor spaces to the outdoors.

ii. Skylights and Clerestory Windows: Add skylights or high-mounted windows to brighten rooms while maintaining privacy.

iii. Reflective Surfaces: Incorporate mirrors and light-colored finishes to amplify natural light.

4. Choose a Cohesive Design Style

Select a design style that complements the industrial and rustic origins of a barndominium while reflecting your personality.

i. Modern Industrial: Embrace exposed metal beams, polished concrete floors, and minimalist furniture for a clean, modern look.

ii. Rustic Farmhouse: Use warm wood finishes, shiplap walls, and vintage accents to create a cozy, traditional vibe.

iii. Contemporary Minimalist: Incorporate sleek lines, neutral tones, and open spaces for a sophisticated, minimalist feel.

iv. Blended Styles: Mix elements from multiple styles to create a unique, personalized interior. For example, combine modern furniture with rustic wood accents.

5. Focus on Key Rooms

1. Kitchen: The kitchen is often the centerpiece of a barndominium, especially in open-concept layouts.

    i.   Island or Peninsula: Include an island or peninsula to provide extra counter space and define the kitchen within an open floor plan.

   ii.   Custom Cabinetry: Opt for built-in cabinets that maximize storage while aligning with your design style.

  iii.   Energy-Efficient Appliances: Install modern, energy-efficient appliances to save on utility costs and enhance functionality.

2. Living Room

    i.   Central Gathering Area: Arrange furniture around a focal point, such as a fireplace, TV, or large window.

ii.   Comfortable Seating: Choose a mix of seating options (e.g., sofas, armchairs, and ottomans) to create a welcoming space.

iii.   Layered Lighting: Use overhead lighting, floor lamps, and wall sconces to adjust brightness for different occasions.

3. Bedrooms

i.   Privacy and Comfort: Position bedrooms away from high-traffic areas to maintain quiet and privacy.

ii.   Built-In Closets: Maximize space with walk-in or built-in closets.

iii.   Lofted Bedrooms: In smaller barndominiums, consider lofted bedrooms to save floor space.

4. Bathrooms

i.   Functional Layout: Place bathrooms near bedrooms and high-traffic areas for convenience.

ii.   Luxurious Features: Include modern features like a walk-in shower, soaking tub, or double vanity.

iii.   Storage: Add recessed shelves or cabinetry for toiletries and towels.

5. Home Office or Workspace

i.   Multi-Functional Design: Dedicate a corner of the living area or a loft space to a home office or hobby area.

ii.   Soundproofing: Use rugs, curtains, and partitions to minimize noise for work or creative spaces.

6. Garage or Workshop

i.   Separate Entry: Design a separate entrance for the garage or workshop to keep workspaces distinct from living areas.

ii.   Custom Storage: Include built-in shelving, pegboards, or cabinets to organize tools and equipment.

6. Select Durable and Functional Materials

Barndominiums are versatile spaces, so choosing durable materials is important, especially for families or those incorporating workshops or garages.

Flooring:

- Concrete floors for durability and a modern look.
- Vinyl or laminate for a budget-friendly, water-resistant option.
- Hardwood or engineered wood for warmth and elegance.

Walls and Ceilings:

- Shiplap or reclaimed wood for a rustic touch.
- Drywall for a clean, traditional look.
- Exposed metal beams or panels for industrial flair.

Counters and Surfaces:

Quartz or granite countertops for long-lasting beauty and resilience.

Butcher block for a farmhouse aesthetic.

7. Add Custom Touches

Personalize your barndominium with design elements that reflect your taste and lifestyle.

- Accent Walls: Create a focal point with bold paint colors, wallpaper, or reclaimed wood.
- Sliding Barn Doors: Add charm and save space with sliding barn doors in bedrooms, bathrooms, or pantries.
- Built-In Shelving: Incorporate custom shelving for books, décor, or functional storage.
- Fireplace or Stove: Consider a wood-burning stove or modern fireplace as a cozy centerpiece for the living area.

8. Plan for Energy Efficiency and Comfort

- Insulation: Use high-quality insulation (spray foam, fiberglass) to regulate indoor temperatures and reduce energy costs.
- Windows and Doors: Install energy-efficient windows and doors to minimize heat loss or gain.
- HVAC Systems: Choose an energy-efficient heating and cooling system that suits the size of your barndominium.

9. Optimize for Storage

Storage is key in maintaining a clean and functional home.

- Hidden Storage: Use under-bed storage, built-in cabinets, or storage benches to make the most of your space.
- Pantry: Include a walk-in or built-in pantry in the kitchen for food and small appliances.

- Garage Storage: Add shelves, cabinets, or ceiling racks in your garage or workshop.

10. Incorporate Outdoor Living

Extend your living space to the outdoors for added functionality and enjoyment.

- Covered Porches: Design a porch for relaxing, dining, or entertaining.
- Patios and Decks: Use concrete, wood, or stone to create an outdoor seating or grilling area.
- Large Doors: Sliding glass or French doors can connect indoor and outdoor spaces seamlessly.

Designing the interior of your barndominium is an exciting opportunity to create a space that is both functional and personalized. Start with a practical layout that suits your lifestyle, then incorporate durable materials, natural light, and custom touches to bring your vision to life.

Chapter 11

Systems in Your Barndominium

The plumbing, electrical, and HVAC (heating, ventilation, and air conditioning) systems are critical components of your barndominium that ensure functionality, comfort, and safety. Proper installation and planning are essential to avoid future issues and to comply with local building codes. Here's a detailed guide to help you understand these systems and make informed decisions during your construction process.

1. Plumbing Systems

Plumbing involves water supply, drainage, and waste management systems for your barndominium. Proper planning and installation ensure water flow and sanitation while preventing leaks or system failures.

Planning Your Plumbing System

- Blueprint Design: Work with a plumber or engineer to create a blueprint that includes water supply lines, drainpipes, and fixture locations (e.g., sinks, toilets, showers).
- Local Codes: Research and comply with local plumbing codes to avoid fines or delays during inspections.

Water Supply Options:

- Municipal Water: Connect to a city water line if available.
- Well Water: Drill a private well if your property isn't near municipal water services.

Drainage and Waste Systems:

- Municipal Sewage: Connect to the city sewer system if available.
- Septic Tank: Install a septic system with adequate capacity for your household size.

- Greywater Systems: For sustainability, consider a greywater system to reuse water for irrigation.

Installation Process

- Water Supply Lines: Install durable materials such as PEX (cross-linked polyethylene) or copper pipes for longevity and resistance to freezing.
- Drainage Pipes: Use PVC or ABS pipes for effective waste removal. Ensure proper slope for gravity-fed drains.
- Fixtures: Rough-in plumbing for sinks, showers, tubs, and toilets before walls are finished.
- Water Heater: Choose between traditional tank heaters or energy-efficient tankless systems.
- Inspections: Schedule inspections during rough-in and final stages to ensure compliance.

gauge for outlets). Protect wiring in metal or plastic conduit where required.

- Breaker Panel: Mount the breaker panel and connect circuits for specific areas (e.g., kitchen, living room, HVAC). Clearly label circuits for easy identification.
- Inspection: Electrical inspections are required after rough-in wiring and upon completion. Ensure all connections are secure and meet code standards.

3. HVAC Systems

The HVAC system maintains a comfortable temperature, regulates humidity, and ensures good air quality. Proper installation is crucial for energy efficiency and comfort.

Planning Your HVAC System

System Size: Choose an appropriately sized system for your barndominium. An HVAC professional will calculate this based on the square footage, insulation, and local climate.

Ductwork Layout: Plan the placement of ducts and vents to ensure even airflow throughout the home.

Zoning: Consider zoning systems that allow different temperature settings for separate areas (e.g., bedrooms vs. living areas).

Types of HVAC Systems

1. Central HVAC:

- Pros: Provides even heating and cooling throughout the house.
- Cons: Requires ductwork, which can be more expensive and less efficient if not sealed properly.

2. Mini-Split Systems:

- Pros: Energy-efficient and allows for zoning. No ductwork is required.

- Cons: Higher upfront costs for installation.

3. Heat Pumps:

- Pros: Energy-efficient for both heating and cooling.
- Cons: Less effective in extreme cold without supplemental heating.

4. Radiant Floor Heating:

- Pros: Provides consistent, energy-efficient heat for large spaces.
- Cons: Expensive and time-intensive to install, often requiring it to be done before flooring is installed.

Installation Process

- Ductwork Installation: Install ductwork in walls, ceilings, or crawl spaces. Seal joints to prevent air leaks.

- Vents and Registers: Place vents strategically to allow even airflow and avoid obstructions.

- Unit Installation: Install HVAC units in designated areas, such as utility closets, basements, or outdoor spaces for condensers.

- Thermostats: Install programmable or smart thermostats for better temperature control and energy efficiency.

Tips for Seamless Integration

1. Coordinate with Contractors: Ensure that plumbers, electricians, and HVAC professionals communicate to avoid overlapping work or system conflicts.

2. Plan Early: Design layouts for plumbing, electrical, and HVAC systems before framing begins to ensure proper placement of pipes, wiring, and ducts.

3. Future-Proof Systems: Install systems that can accommodate future needs, such as additional appliances, smart home features, or expansions.

4. Energy Efficiency: Invest in energy-efficient systems and materials to reduce long-term utility costs. Look for ENERGY STAR-rated appliances, proper insulation, and sealed ductwork.

5. Schedule Inspections: Have inspections conducted at rough-in and final stages for each system to ensure compliance with building codes.

Cost Considerations

1. Plumbing: $5,000–$10,000 for an average-sized barndominium, depending on complexity and fixtures.
2. Electrical: $3,000–$8,000 depending on the size of the house, number of circuits, and smart features.

3. HVAC: $5,000–$15,000 depending on system type, size, and ductwork requirements.

Plumbing, electrical, and HVAC systems are essential to making your barndominium functional and comfortable. Careful planning, professional installation, and adherence to local building codes will ensure these systems operate efficiently and safely.

Chapter 12

Landscaping and Exterior Design for Your Barndominium

The landscaping and exterior design of your barndominium play a key role in creating a functional and visually appealing property. Thoughtful planning can enhance curb appeal, improve usability, and seamlessly integrate your barndominium into its natural surroundings. Whether you're aiming for a rustic, modern, or minimalist style, landscaping and exterior elements can help bring your vision to life.

1. Exterior Design Features

The exterior of your barndominium should be both attractive and practical, reflecting your personal style while being durable and weather-resistant.

Siding and Finishes

- Metal Siding: A popular choice for barndominiums due to its durability, low maintenance, and industrial charm.
- Wood Accents: Use reclaimed wood, shiplap, or cedar to add a warm, rustic feel.
- Stone or Brick Veneer: Add texture and elegance with stone or brick accents around the base, entryway, or columns.
- Paint Colors: Neutral tones like gray, white, or beige are versatile, while bold colors like barn red or navy can add personality.

Roofing Options

- Metal Roofs: Durable and weather-resistant, they are ideal for both rustic and modern designs.
- Solar Panels: Incorporate solar panels to reduce energy costs and enhance sustainability.

Windows and Doors

- Oversized Windows: Maximize natural light and connect the interior to the outdoors.
- Sliding or French Doors: These can provide access to patios, decks, or gardens while enhancing the look of the exterior.
- Barn Doors: Add charm to your exterior design, especially for garages or storage areas.

Covered Porches and Patios

- Create functional outdoor spaces for relaxing, dining, or entertaining.
- Use pergolas, overhangs, or wrap-around porches to provide shade and protect entrances from the elements.

2. Landscaping Ideas

Landscaping enhances the visual appeal and functionality of your property. It's also an opportunity to tie the natural surroundings to the design of your barndominium.

Front Yard Design

- Pathways: Create walkways leading to the entrance using gravel, stone, or stamped concrete for a welcoming look.
- Plant Beds: Frame your entrance with flowerbeds, shrubs, or ornamental grasses. Use native plants for low-maintenance, eco-friendly landscaping.
- Lighting: Install pathway lighting, uplighting for trees, or string lights for a cozy, inviting atmosphere.

Backyard and Outdoor Spaces

- Decks and Patios: Build a deck or patio for outdoor seating, dining, or relaxing.
- Fire Pit or Fireplace: Add a fire pit or outdoor fireplace to create a social gathering space.

- Garden Spaces: Design vegetable or flower gardens to add color and productivity to your yard.

Driveways and Parking

- Use gravel, asphalt, or concrete for driveways and parking areas.
- Incorporate edging with stones or plants to define spaces.

Water Features

- Consider adding a small pond, fountain, or waterfall for a peaceful ambiance.
- Use rain barrels to collect water for irrigation, enhancing sustainability.

3. Sustainable Landscaping

For environmentally conscious homeowners, sustainable landscaping can reduce maintenance and promote biodiversity.

- Native Plants: Use plants native to your region for low water and fertilizer needs.
- Rain Gardens: Direct runoff water into landscaped areas with water-loving plants to reduce erosion.
- Drought-Tolerant Landscaping: Incorporate xeriscaping techniques using rocks, mulch, and drought-resistant plants.
- Composting: Set up a composting area to recycle organic waste and improve soil health.

4. Fencing and Boundaries

Fencing can serve both aesthetic and functional purposes, such as defining property lines, providing privacy, or keeping animals secure.

- Wooden Fences: Offer a rustic or farmhouse aesthetic and can be stained or painted to match the exterior.

- Metal Fences: Durable and low-maintenance, perfect for a modern or industrial look.
- Hedgerows: Use natural hedges or shrubs to create a living fence for privacy or noise reduction.

5. Outdoor Amenities

Consider adding outdoor amenities to enhance the functionality of your barndominium property.

- Outdoor Kitchens: Include a grill, countertop, sink, and seating area for entertaining.
- Recreational Spaces: Install a pool, basketball court, or play area for family activities.
- Storage Buildings: Add barns, sheds, or workshops to store equipment, tools, or recreational items.

- Animal Shelters: If you have livestock or pets, include shelters, corrals, or dog runs.

6. Low-Maintenance Landscaping Tips

- Mulch Beds: Use mulch around plants to retain moisture and suppress weeds.
- Drip Irrigation: Install a drip irrigation system for efficient watering with minimal effort.
- Artificial Turf: For areas that don't require live grass, use artificial turf to reduce mowing and watering needs.
- Perennials: Plant perennials that come back year after year, reducing the need for replanting.

7. Lighting and Security

Outdoor lighting enhances safety and creates ambiance for your barndominium's exterior.

- Pathway Lighting: Install lights along walkways and driveways for visibility at night.
- Motion Sensor Lights: Add security with motion-activated lights around entrances and garages.
- Accent Lighting: Use spotlights to highlight architectural features or landscaping elements.

8. Maintenance Considerations

- Design your landscaping and exterior features with long-term maintenance in mind.
- Choose materials like metal, composite decking, and gravel that are durable and weather-resistant.
- Use automated irrigation systems to minimize manual watering.

- Keep a consistent schedule for tasks like mowing, pruning, and cleaning gutters to preserve your property's appearance.

Chapter 13

Living in and Maintaining Your Barndominium

Barndominiums are designed to provide comfort, durability, and functionality, making them a popular choice for modern homeowners. However, like any home, living in a barndominium requires attention to maintenance and upkeep to ensure it remains a safe and enjoyable space for years to come. Proper care not only preserves its structural integrity but also protects your investment. Here's a guide to living in and maintaining your barndominium effectively.

1. Adapting to Barndominium Living

Living in a barndominium combines the charm of rustic living with the convenience of modern amenities.

- Open Floor Plans: Take advantage of the spacious design by using furniture and décor to define areas like the living room, kitchen, and dining spaces.

- Energy Efficiency: Insulation and energy-efficient windows reduce utility costs. Consider upgrading to smart thermostats and LED lighting to maximize savings.
- Multi-Functional Spaces: Barndominiums often include integrated garages, workshops, or storage areas. Keep these spaces organized to maintain functionality.
- Outdoor Living: Many barndominiums feature patios, porches, or open land. Use these areas to extend your living space with outdoor furniture or recreational features.

2. General Maintenance Tips

Regular maintenance keeps your barndominium in good condition and prevents small issues from turning into costly repairs.

A. Exterior Maintenance

1. Metal Siding and Roof:

- Clean metal surfaces annually with a mild detergent to remove dirt, mold, or debris.
- Check for rust or corrosion, especially in areas exposed to water, and apply touch-up paint or rust inhibitors as needed.

2. Gutters and Downspouts:

- Clean gutters at least twice a year to prevent water buildup and foundation damage.
- Ensure downspouts direct water away from the foundation to prevent pooling.

3. Windows and Doors:

- Inspect seals and weatherstripping for cracks or wear. Replace them to maintain energy efficiency.
- Clean glass regularly and lubricate hinges and locks for smooth operation.

B. Interior Maintenance

1. Walls and Ceilings:

- Inspect drywall or paneling for cracks or damage, especially near joints or seams. Repair as needed.
- If your barndominium features exposed beams or metal panels, clean them periodically to prevent dust buildup.

2. Floors:

- Protect flooring with rugs or mats in high-traffic areas.
- Use appropriate cleaners for the type of flooring (e.g., concrete, laminate, wood) to avoid damage.

3. Plumbing:

- Check for leaks under sinks, around toilets, and near water heaters. Address any issues promptly to avoid water damage.

- Flush water heaters annually to remove sediment buildup.

3. Climate-Specific Maintenance

Barndominiums, like all homes, are subject to weather-related wear and tear.

1. Cold Climates:

- Insulate pipes to prevent freezing.
- Check the roof and gutters for ice dams or snow buildup.

2. Hot Climates:

- Inspect insulation and HVAC systems regularly to ensure they can handle high temperatures.
- Use UV-resistant coatings or shades to protect windows and exterior surfaces.

3. Humid Climates:

- Monitor for mold or mildew in areas prone to moisture, such as bathrooms or basements.
- Use dehumidifiers or ventilation systems to control indoor humidity.

4. HVAC System Care

Heating, ventilation, and air conditioning systems are vital for maintaining a comfortable living environment.

- Replace air filters every 1–3 months to keep the system running efficiently.
- Schedule annual inspections to ensure the system is operating correctly and to address any issues before they escalate.
- Clean vents and ductwork periodically to improve air quality and system performance.

5. Preventative Maintenance

Taking a proactive approach to maintenance saves time and money in the long run.

- Regular Inspections: Conduct semi-annual inspections of your barndominium's structure, roof, plumbing, and electrical systems.
- Sealant and Caulking: Check and reapply caulk around windows, doors, and siding to maintain a tight seal and prevent water or air leaks.

Pest Control:

- Inspect for signs of pests like termites, rodents, or ants.
- Seal cracks or openings in the exterior to prevent infestations.

6. Protecting Your Barndominium Investment

1. Energy Efficiency Upgrades

- Insulation: Maintain proper insulation to reduce energy costs and improve indoor comfort. Consider upgrading to spray foam for better efficiency.

- Solar Panels: Invest in solar panels to offset electricity costs and improve sustainability.
- Energy-Efficient Appliances: Replace outdated appliances with ENERGY STAR-certified models.

2. Insurance and Warranty

- Ensure your barndominium is covered by a comprehensive insurance policy that includes coverage for natural disasters, fire, and liability.
- Keep warranties for roofing, siding, and HVAC systems in case repairs or replacements are needed.

7. Keeping the Exterior Functional and Beautiful

1. Landscaping

- Drainage: Maintain proper drainage around the property to prevent erosion and water pooling near the foundation.

- Plant Maintenance: Trim trees and shrubs regularly to keep them from damaging siding, windows, or the roof.
- Seasonal Cleanup: Remove fallen leaves, snow, or debris to keep walkways and outdoor areas safe and functional.

2. Outdoor Features

Porches and Decks:

- Inspect for rot or structural issues, especially in wood decking.
- Reseal or repaint surfaces every 2–3 years to protect against the elements.

Fencing and Driveways:

- Repair any damaged fencing or gate mechanisms.
- Fill cracks in driveways or parking areas to prevent further deterioration.

8. Sustainability and Long-Term Planning

Sustainable Living

- Rainwater Collection: Use rain barrels to collect water for irrigation.
- Composting: Set up a compost bin for organic waste and use it to enrich your garden soil.

Future Expansion

- Plan for possible future expansions, such as adding additional living space, workshops, or outdoor amenities.

Conclusively; Building a barndominium is not just about constructing a home, it's about creating a space that reflects your personality, supports your lifestyle, and gives you a sense of pride and accomplishment. While the process may seem challenging at times, the reward is well worth the effort.

Take things one step at a time, lean on the expertise of others, and remember that you're capable of completing this incredible project. At the end of the journey, you'll not only have a one-of-a-kind home but also the satisfaction of knowing you brought your dream to life. Stay focused, enjoy the process, and trust in your vision. Your dream barndominium is within reach!

Made in United States
North Haven, CT
29 May 2025

69295363R00114